PUTTING AN END TO
WORSHIP
WARS

PUTTING AN END TO
WORSHIP
WARS

UNDERSTANDING:

WHY PEOPLE DISAGREE OVER WORSHIP

THE SIX BASIC WORSHIP STYLES

HOW TO FIND BALANCE AND MAKE PEACE

ELMER TOWNS

BROADMAN
& HOLMAN
PUBLISHERS

Nashville, Tennessee

Published by Broadman & Holman Publishers,
Nashville, Tennessee
Acquisitions & Development Editor: John Landers
Page Design and Typography: TF Designs, Mt. Juliet, Tennessee
Printed in the United States of America

4230-17
0-8054-3017-2

Dewey Decimal Classification: 264
Subject Heading: PUBLIC WORSHIP
Library of Congress Card Catalog Number: 96-27811

Unless otherwise noted, Scripture quotations are from the New King
James Version of the Bible, © 1979, 1980, 1982, Thomas Nelson, Inc.,
Publishers. Verses marked NIV are from the Holy Bible, New Interna-
tional Version, copyright © 1973, 1978, 1984 by International Bible
Society.

Library of Congress Cataloging-in-Publication Data
Towns, Elmer L.
  Putting an end to worship wars / Elmer Towns.
    p. cm.
  ISBN 0-8054-3017-2 (pbk.)
  1. Public worship. 2. Church attendance. 3. Church membership.
4. Choice of church. 5. Evangelistic work. 6. Popular culture—Religious aspects—Christianity. 7. Christianity and culture. I. Title.
  BV15.T68   1997
  264'.001—dc20

                                                96-27811
                                                CIP

97 98 99 00 01 5 4 3

Contents

PART THREE
Principles to Remember

Appendixes

Preface

I wrote this book immediately after delivering the Lyman Stewart Lectures at Talbot Theological Seminary (LaMirada, Calif., Oct. 24–26, 1995) on the topic "New Paradigms in Church Worship, Evangelism, and Education." There was intense interest by the student body; they realized the tension between the contemporary worship expressions they prefer and the traditional worship of their parents.

In the summer of 1995 I attended the Missouri Lutheran Conference in Orlando, Florida, and spoke on the "Changing Paradigms of Church Worship," sponsored by the Lutheran Church, Missouri Synod. I was asked whether the new seeker-sensitive worship expressions emerging in some Missouri Lutheran churches is biblical. I told them the new seeker worship services do express biblical principles, and I encouraged the young minister using this new worship format. Some older ministers did not like my opinion; they were pleased, however, when I said the older Lutheran liturgy expressed biblical principles. I pointed out the new seeker services could be superficial and frothy, hence, unbiblical. Likewise, the old Lutheran liturgy could be dead and meaningless, also unbiblical.

The essence of my addresses at Talbot Theological Seminary and to the Missouri Lutheran ministers is in this book. While the thoughts of this book have been developing for twenty years, I am grateful to Broadman & Holman for giving me an opportunity to put them into printed expression for others to examine.

I want to thank my secretary, Linda Elliott, for typing and proofreading the manuscript. My friend and long-time research assistant, Dr. Doug Porter, helped gather data for this volume. His commitment to the health and growth of the church has been an inspiration to me. This book is the product of many who have influenced my thinking and contributed to my ministry. I give credit to so many who have influenced my life, but in the final analysis, I bear responsibility for all of the omissions and weaknesses. May God overlook them and use this book to produce effective churches with worshiping members who weekly touch God, and are touched by God.

Introduction

Worship is not an elective for a Christian who has enrolled in the school of Christ; it is a required course. Jesus said, "The Father seeketh such [sincere worshipers] to worship him" (John 4:23, KJV); therefore, the child of God must respond by giving glory to God.

The fact of worship is the focus of this book, not its methodology or how to plan a worship service. This is not a prescriptive book that a leader follows to plan a worship service. It is a descriptive book that reflects the trends and tensions in our contemporary church over worship practices.

A discouraged typical contemporary pastor may attend a conference and experience a different worship style from the way he does it back home. When the floundering pastor feels the excitement of new worship experiences, he concludes, "We need worship excitement in our church," so he begins to make plans to change the current worship format.

The pastor has gone through the internal process of revitalizing his worship style. Because the old is unfulfilling and the new is tantalizing he is ready to change.

Back home he introduces a new format on Sunday morning. Some people like it; some people don't. Some are uncomfortable; some people eagerly follow the pastor in new expressions of worship. If the worship makeover is universally accepted by the congregation, there will be no problems; but if everyone is unhappy, there will be tensions for him and the church.

Eventually, resistance to new worship forms will manifest itself in several ways. A few isolated individuals may stop attending, or they may move their membership elsewhere. Some never complain or instigate trouble; they usually just disappear.

A few agitators might cluster together to reinforce one another. They find common irritation for complaint; they begin voicing their feelings. This group may leave the church, creating a "church split" if they are large enough, or a "church splinter" if they are a small minority. They may attempt to rally support to force the pastor to return to the former ways of worship (i.e., that which is comfortable or familiar to them). If they can't get their way, they may begin a campaign to remove the pastor.

"Let's hire a pastor who will lead us the way God wants us to worship," they say. What they really mean is "Let's hire a pastor to do what we want."

Does the pastor have the authority to change the worship style of the people? Does he have authority to take away the form of worship they have always followed in worshiping God? Do the people have the authority to rebel against their pastor, who is attempting to revitalize an ineffective worship service?

A pastor must realize that the church belongs to the people, for it is the body of Christ on earth; and because we belong to Him, we are all members one of another. The people must realize the pastor's task is to lead sheep, feed sheep, and protect sheep (Acts 20:28–30). If the worship service is dull and nonproductive, it is the pastor's responsibility to revitalize the worship experience so that when worshipers enter the house of God, they feel His presence and hear His voice.

Both leader and worshiper face difficult questions. This book doesn't have all the answers, but it raises questions:

- What do you do in worship?
- How do you worship?
- What motivates you to worship?
- What are the results of worship?

The effectiveness of worship is not measured by atmosphere, or by how fast the songs are sung, or how deeply we meditate in solitude. It is not measured by a new Plexiglas pulpit, a split-chancel pulpit, or the new trend of using no pulpit at all. It is not measured by raising hands, by affirming the Apostles' Creed, or by congregational applause. It is not measured by responsive readings from both Old and New Testament, by viewing The Living Bible projected on the screen, or by listening to an expositional sermon based on a proper interpretation of the text.

True worship is always measured by the response of the believer's heart to God. Those who worship God must give Him the "worthship" that is due to Him.

True worship is measured by the transformation of worshipers because they have been in the presence of God. It is measured by repentance because worshipers have faced their sins and asked forgiveness. It is measured by new insights about God that deepen their daily walk with God.

True worship upsets the way we have lived and demands more sacrifice from the worshipers. True worship never allows us to remain the same person we were before we came into the presence of God.

True worship involves change, and it also includes that which never changes. We must be careful that we don't get the two mixed up. It is we who change because we have been in the presence of an unchanging God. He doesn't adapt Himself to us; we adapt ourselves to Him because we yield to Him, we obey Him, we magnify Him, and we lift Him up.

The unchanging nature of worship doesn't mean we never change our forms of worship, nor does it mean we never rearrange the order of service. Because worship is a response to God—and He never changes—then there are certain "self-evident truths" in worship that cannot be manipulated. It is imperative that we worship God in truth (John 4:23), which is the substance of worship. It is not imperative whether methods of communicating truth be a Bible expositional sermon, an evangelistic presentation of the gospel, or a pastor's exhortation to godliness. It is imperative that we worship Him in spirit (John 4:23), which is the sincere expression of our hearts. It is not imperative whether we express it with reverently bowed heads, raised hands of praise, or shouts of "Hallelujah!"

Worship is like a car to get us from where we are to where God wants us to be. Transportation and communication are imperative; the mode or vehicle is not imperative. Some worship God in cathedrals with the rich traditional organ tones of Bach and Fauré from the classics of Europe. They travel in a Mercedes Benz. Some worship God in simple wooden churches with a steeple pointing heavenward. They sing the gospel songs of Charles Wesley or Fanny Crosby. They travel in a Ford or Chevy. Some worship God with the contemporary sounds of praise music with a gentle beat. They travel in a convertible sports coupe. Some worship God to the whine of a guitar and the amplifiers to the max. They travel on a motorcycle, without a muffler.

Six expressions of worship will be analyzed in this book. Rather than prescribing any one of the worship expressions, each will be described. This book does not focus on methodology (how to successfully conduct a worship service), but it makes some suggestions at the end of each of the six worship expressions.

How to Read This Book

I am not writing this book to change your worship style. Congregations resist change, and even lay leaders will resist change if they are not fully persuaded. So let's proceed with the assumption you will not change your worship format. Why should you not change? Worship is not legitimate unless it comes from the heart. When you change your form of worship for convenience or to be more successful, it's not from the heart. Like Esau, you've sold your birthright for a mess of pottage.

As you read this book, think of walking into an art gallery to study six beautiful masterpiece paintings, each picture reflecting the skill and feelings of the master painter who poured his soul onto canvas. Try to see what is there. Don't just try to disprove their validity, rather examine the Scriptures to see where each conforms to biblical mandates. Just as you would examine an oil painting—interpreting its mixture of colors and shadows, its presentation of personality and moods, its reflection of culture and tradition—try to see the world through the eyes of worshipers who express themselves differently than you.

Now, return to your worship style and do it better. Don't change for the sake of someone else's model. Do what God has called you to do. Learn from others, and improve yourself, and revitalize your church.

Remember, when you look over the fence at someone else's greener worship grass, they may be looking admiringly at the benefits of grazing in your worship pasture. Improvement, like beauty, may be in the eyes of the beholder.

These six worship styles are different from each other, and each is different from other churches in their neighborhood. For example, not all liturgical churches worship the exact same way. Since churches are the composite expression of many people, and people are constantly growing, learning, and changing, so their worship expression is constantly growing, expanding, and changing.

Each church that reflects a worship expression is probably different than it was a few years ago. Each church probably changed to meet the needs of its worshipers, as its worshipers changed it. They changed the tones of worship, the order of service, the type of music, even the style of preaching to better communicate with growing people who are represented in our churches.

Many Americans have changed their place of worship, not like the Europeans who tend to remain in one building generation after generation. And by internal desires, we redecorate our sanctuaries, changing the color of paint, carpets, and lighting in the rooms in which we worship. We change the flowers with the seasons and the music to express the tradition of our holidays.

The styles of worship in this book have a lot to say about the American church scene. Jack Hayford, pastor of the Church on the Way, Van Nuys, California, says we are experiencing more than a change in worship; it's a reformation of worship.[1] He claims the first reformation under Martin Luther was a reformation of doctrine, doing away with Roman Catholic doctrine. Now he maintains there must be a reformation of worship, doing away with European or Roman Catholic liturgy. Hayford wants a reformation in worship to reflect his form of worship—a renewal worship service with emphasis on charismatic expression. I agree with Hayford's view that we are experiencing a reformation of worship, but I maintain that just as there were several expressions of theological systems in the Protestant Reformation (e.g., Lutheranism, Calvinism, Armenianism, and eventually Wesleyism), so today there are several contemporary expressions in today's worship reformation (e.g., Bible Expositional, Body Life, Renewal).

This book is not written just as an academic expression, nor is it a response to a contemporary problem in the church. It is the result of a life-long pilgrimage. May you take this pilgrimage with me and be driven back to the Word of God to rediscover your foundation. Anchor yourself in the Rock of Ages. May the insights of this book give you more confidence in ministry than ever before.

PART ONE

Current Tension over Worship

CHAPTER ONE

New Worship Styles

Worship shapes the human community in response to the living God. If worship is neglected or perverted, our communities fall into chaos or under tyranny.

Eugene Peterson, *The Message*

Historically, when Protestant church members moved their home from one location to the next, they usually chose a new local church on the basis of doctrine, not on the basis of worship style. While the style of worship was important to them, doctrine was the final criterion. The priorities were (1) doctrine, (2) the name of the church, and (3) denominational alliance.[1]

Most denominations had the same style of worship that went with people's denominational or doctrinal loyalty. Presbyterians tended to choose a Presbyterian church when they moved, and if one was not available, they would choose a church with reformed theology. But even stretched to the limits, Presbyterians would probably not have chosen a church with pentecostal or Arminian beliefs. One would have expected them to choose a church that at least held a similar view of eternal security.

Denominational alignment meant people were comfortable with a church's heritage, lifestyle, or policies. This included the worship style that was reflected in their individual churches. In the past, most denominations were not influenced by inter-denominational television services and by ministers trained in interde-nominational seminaries. Because

> ### How People Historically Have Chosen a Church
> 1. Doctrine
> 2. Name
> 3. Denomination

denominations were relatively homogeneous, people could transfer from one church to another and fit in rather comfortably because there was little difference from one congregation to another. Their worship expectations were usually fulfilled.

Americans generally have not been quick to choose a church with a non-standardized name. People have chosen churches with names that tended to be as acceptable as "mainline" names: Methodist, Presbyterian, Baptist, Episcopal, or Lutheran. Everyone knew what these names reflected. Historically, nonacceptable names to people from mainline churches were Holiness, Temple, Pentecostal, Nazarene, Mennonite, or a Bible church. To mainliners these names represented a sect, an unknown entity or an outcast group. People didn't know what to expect when they visited the worship service in these churches.

Contemporary Worship

Today, Americans are not as choosy about church names. Now they choose a church primarily by its style of worship or its philosophy of ministry. People are not looking for denominational labels, doctrine, or a predetermined name. Presbyterians are not necessarily looking for a church that has covenant theology or reformed doctrine or that has *Presbyterian* in its name. They may attend and join a charismatic renewal church because they enjoy clapping, lifting their hands, or singing praise choruses. They

> ### Demands of American Culture Forced on the Church
> 1. User-friendly access
> 2. Participatory services
> 3. Experiential involvement
> 4. Electronic amplification
> 5. Contemporary music
> 6. Options of worship time
> 7. Choice of different worship experiences

may feel this is the way God should be worshiped. So they sublimate their doctrinal preferences and abandon their tradition for a new philosophy of worship.

What is the primary source of this change? It is coming from without the church, not within. Culture is influencing the church more than the church is influencing the culture.

What is in our culture that is influencing the way Americans choose churches? It seems to be no single experience but the whole thrust of society.

America has become a consumer society, driven by marketing, advertising, and retailing. Everything is sold—groceries, clothing, furniture, cars, entertainment. Consumerism is the engine that drives American society, and it is the driving force as Americans choose their churches (but that doesn't make it right).

The Glue of Culture

In the early 1800s, America was an agricultural society, with 92 percent of Americans living and working on the farm. With the Industrial Revolution of the 1840s people moved to the cities, and American culture evolved from a rural society into an urban industrial society to provide jobs and income. The nation became one of the world's largest producers of steel, cars, and machinery.

After World War II, America changed again. We were no longer a producing society, but we became a consumer society. Now the glue that holds our culture together is marketing, selling, and buying. Less than 25 percent of our society is employed to produce or manufacture something. Less than 5 percent work on a farm.

Our favorite pastime seems to be walking the malls, not necessarily to purchase necessities but just to shop. We look for trinkets, what is new, or just the experience of seeing new things. We buy what is comfortable, enjoyable, flattering, or entertaining.

In the same way, America's Protestants choose churches on the basis of what entertains us, satisfies us, or makes us feel good about God and ourselves. And, to a growing degree, this freedom of choice is also the reason some Roman Catholics and even some persons from non-Christian religions switch to Protestant churches.

If we recognize church worshipers as consumers, we will recognize church programs as menus, and types of worship as the main entrees in a restaurant. Consumers go where the menu fits their taste. Americans can pick from an abundance of options: Chinese, Mexican, fried chicken, pizza, hamburgers, and so on.

A similar variety of consumer options is available when it comes to churches. The worship menus are not filled with doctrinal options but with a variety of worship options. Americans worship where they feel comfortable with the style of expression that best reflects their inclinations and temperament:

- A Lutheran couple chooses a charismatic renewal church because they like positive exaltation. Perhaps they thought their former Lutheran church was lifeless.
- A Baptist leaves the revivalistic Baptist church to attend a Bible expositional church because he feels his former church was superficial and the new church has in-depth teaching.
- A Pentecostal leaves the church of his birth claiming that "wildfire" has no place in his life. He chooses a meditative liturgical church experience in a Lutheran or Episcopal church where the atmospheric worship experience enables him to stand in awe of the majesty of God.
- The Salvation Army sergeant leaves the familiar surroundings of the citadel to make new relationships in the small groups of a Body-Life Church.

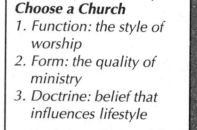

How People Currently Choose a Church
1. Function: the style of worship
2. Form: the quality of ministry
3. Doctrine: belief that influences lifestyle

No matter what the style of worship, there seems to be a two-way door in and out of most sanctuaries. New people are entering to seek its strength, while others, tired of the routine, are leaving to seek their Sunday morning "high" elsewhere. So the old phrase "the church of your choice" no longer means your doctrinal choice; rather, it reflects your style of life and your way of worshiping God.

While these motives are negative factors in our churches because they minimize the doctrines taught in the Word of God, there is one plus: more nonchurch people are coming to our worship services than in previous years. When people search out churches where they find meaning or where their life's goals are supported, consumerism has resulted in an open door for evangelism.

Styles of Worship and Ministry

Historically, there have been two basic worship styles in the Protestant church since the Reformation: "high church" and "low church." To describe them functionally we might refer to them as the liturgical worship service and the congregational style of worship.

Liturgical worship usually follows a printed order of events that include the Invocation, Doxology, the Lord's Prayer, choir anthems, responsive reading of Scripture, choral response to the pastoral prayer, the Gloria Patri, and the singing of "Amen" at the end of each hymn. Many believe the atmospheric worship of the Liturgical Church service expresses New Testament Christianity. Historically, there have not been many voices to challenge the credibility of this worship, but now there are some contemporary voices asking questions about its validity.

The second type of worship has been an expression of the common people in church groups that did not come out of the mainstream of the Reformation (the Anabaptists, Mennonites, Moravians, Puritans, Pilgrims, and others). After the Reformation, this second worship tradition would be followed by such groups as the Methodists, Congregationalists, Baptists, and Brethren.

These groups were usually led by pastors without professional education who preached extemporaneously without a written manuscript. The preaching was emotional, persuasive, and filled with illustrations and the idiomatic language of the common people. "Sweaty preaching" by "plowboy preachers" called for revival and renewal, and, in response, there were tears at the mourners' bench. Singing of gospel songs expressed deep emotion. The services included testimonies, prayers from the laymen, and, in some groups, shouts of "Amen" or "Hallelujah!"

Six Worship Paradigms

Defined by worship styles, six worship types, or paradigms, can now be identified among Protestants:[2] (1) the Evangelistic Church, which focuses on winning the lost; (2) the Bible Expositional Church, which emphasizes teaching the Word of God; (3) the Renewal Church, which focuses on excitement revival and touching God; (4) the Body Life Church, which focuses on fellowship (*koinonia*), relationships, and small groups; (5) the Liturgical Church, which centers on serving and glorifiying God through worship; and (6) the Congregational Church, which has a balanced approach to worship, expressed by the laypeople.

> **Six Worship Styles**
> 1. The Evangelistic Church
> 2. The Bible Expositional Church
> 3. The Renewal Church
> 4. The Body Life Church
> 5. The Liturgical Church
> 6. The Congregational Church

Six distinct philosophies of ministries and/or church growth have emerged in the thinking of church growth authorities. The six models came from their research and observation of the American church scene. At the center of each style of worship are several adhesives, or types of "glue," that hold each church type together. Whereas most Protestant churches will do many of the same things in worship or ministry—pray, sing, collect money, preach, and so on—the way these things are done and the value that worshipers give to them make them distinctive. Each ministry style adds a unique value to one's experience of worship, making it different and, to many, desirable.

The Evangelistic Church

The term *evangelistic* describes a style of ministry that emphasizes such activities as door-to-door visitation for evangelism, the altar call, Sunday school busing, and personal evangelism. These ministries, often called "soul-winning," are prized among an evangelistic church's members.

One example of such a church is Bill Hybels's Willow Creek Community Church of South Barrington, Illinois. (While Hybels disagrees with my assessment, I cannot place his style of church in the other categories.) Hybels calls his Sunday morning service a "seeker service," where the unsaved can feel comfortable, barriers to their salvation are removed, and sermon topics are slanted to their everyday need or experience.

We can find evangelistic-type churches among Presbyterian, Congregational, Pentecostal, Baptist, and other denominations. The doctrine of a denomination is not the determining factor that makes them evangelistic.

The Evangelistic Church usually (1) is action-oriented, as opposed to mediative or instructive; (2) has strong pastor leadership with the spiritual gift of evangelism; (3) has persuasive evangelistic preaching to get people converted; (4) has simplistic organization; (5) is organized to get laypeople involved in outreach; (6) is growth-oriented (numbers-oriented); and (7) is platform-oriented. Usually, the success of the platform ministry of preaching, special music, and the evangelistic appeal will determine the success of the church.

The Bible Expositional Church

This church is usually noted for its use of sermon notes, overhead projectors for people to follow sermon outlines, expository sermons, reference Bibles—such as the Ryrie or Scofield Reference Bible—and constant references to the original languages of the Bible. The dominant spiritual gift of the pastor is teaching. At almost any given service the congregation can be seen taking notes, and many keep the pastor-teacher's presentation in a notebook.

This church usually appeals to the upper-middle class and will usually be found in a college or white-collar community. This type of worship crosses denominational lines and can be found in Baptist, Presbyterian, Methodist, Independent Bible, or a variety of other groups.

The pastor probably learned his preaching style at Dallas Theological Seminary, Talbot Theological Seminary, or some other independent seminary—usually not from a denominational seminary. He might have learned it from some interdenominational organization, such as the Navigators or Campus Crusade for Christ.

The Renewal Church

This church is usually described by its feeling and flow. Worshipers have freedom to lift their hands in worship or clap them in joy. They sing praise choruses, go to the altar to pray, hug one another, and laugh or cry. It is camp meeting and revival every Sunday morning.

They lay hands on one another for healing, power, or anointing. Most of the charismatic churches fall into this category and exercise the miraculous gift of tongues, healing, "word of knowledge," "slain in the spirit," interpretation, or other expressions of the Holy Spirit.

Not all renewal churches are oriented to the pentecostal or charismatic style or express miraculous gifts. I have talked to several Southern Baptist pastors who were being pressured by their local association because of the renewal style in their worship services. These churches were not charismatic in doctrine or pentecostal in lifestyle. The members didn't speak in tongues nor attempt to manifest any of the "sign" gifts. They were Baptist in doctrine and Southern Baptist in allegiance. Sometimes the pressure came from the fact that these churches dropped adult Sunday school and extended the worship service from 10:00 A.M. to noon. The pastors told me they had not changed their doctrine; they were Baptists who supported the Cooperative Program and didn't believe in speaking in tongues, but their worship style was the issue.

Renewal churches can be found among Presbyterian, Episcopal, Roman Catholic, Pentecostal, and the rapidly emerging independent churches.

Theology is not the dividing line; hence, doctrine is not the glue that holds them together. They may preach "power theology," "prosperity theology," pentecostalism, or old-fashioned liberalism. Whatever their thrust, most of them are evangelical in doctrine.

The emphasis in these churches is on personal renewal in fellowship with God. This style of worship is not found in the formal services of a liturgical church, but in the intense experience of pouring out personal love for God.

Whereas formal liturgy emphasizes one-way worship toward God (i.e., giving worship to God that is due Him), worship in the Renewal Church focuses on two-way communication between the person and God. Worshipers must get something out of worship. It must be stimulating, uplifting, and exhilarating. They like worship, and it affirms them. When they go home, they feel good about what they have done.

The Body Life Church

The glue that holds this church together is the relationships that are formed in the small groups, or cells, that make up the body. It is in the small groups where pastoral care happens and people grow spiritually. The Body Life Church has a lot of hugging going on and places value on transparency: being open and honest and caring in their groups. They confess faults to one another, are accountable to one another, and pray for one another.

Body life churches do the other things that normal churches do, such as preach, sing, teach, and worship God. But they prize highly the quality of life they receive from relationships. In a given session they might testify, share burdens, pray for a hurting brother, and share a blessing or an answer to prayer. It is "the body ministering to the body."

The Body Life Church is not a pulpit-dominated church where everyone looks to the pastor for ministry. Instead, a body life church congregation looks to one another for support, help, and ministry. It focuses on *koinonia,* or fellowship, within the body.

Just as in the other cases, body life churches are found in Baptist, Evangelical Free, Independent, or Pentecostal churches. The influence of *koinonia* crosses denominational lines. It is not a church style that is taught in most seminaries, however. Pastors learn it from one another, from conferences, from seminars, or as they intern under a body life church pastor.

The Liturgical Church

In some churches, the style of worship has not changed since the denomination's founding, and people sing the same hymns that were sung by their grandparents. They feel that worship is transcultural and transtemporal. While some feel a liturgical service is dead, others feel invigorated because they know they are obeying God who "seeketh such to worship Him."

Liturgical worshipers do not worship for a feeling. They center all glory, praise, and worship on God. He is the focus of the worship service. The people are not there to evangelize, to learn, to fellowship, or to be renewed. They worship in obedience to God.

The Congregational Church

People want preaching that speaks to them in the Congregational Church. They want sermons that are devotional and motivational, yet also include some teaching, renewal, and worship. The pastor is a shepherd who is one of them and has arisen from them. It is a "low church," in that authority is with the people, rather then being a "high church," where authority is situated at denominational headquarters away from the people.

Early church growth authorities called this a Baptist church because it described churches that were responsible for the entire life of the church; they were self-governing, self-propagating, and self-supporting. However, the present name is the Congregational Church, which identifies many churches that do not have the name "Baptist." A congregational church is where the people are more responsible for the church than the pastor or the denomination. It is a church where the people do the work of ministry in Sunday school, training programs, camps, VBS, and the like. One of the main gifts of the pastor is to organize the people for ministry, rather than doing ministry for them.

Biblical Basis

These six types of worship (also called six paradigms of church growth) represent six basic functions or principles God mandated for the church to carry out. By separating these six functions as dominant characteristics of a church, each model is better understood.

The Evangelistic Church carries out the prescriptive mandate "Go therefore and make disciples of all the nations" (Matt. 28:19). The Evangelistic

Church also is reflected by the descriptive work of the Thessalonians, "From you sounded out the word of the Lord not only in Macedonia and Achaia, but also in every place your faith to God-ward is spread abroad" (1 Thess. 1:8, KJV).

The Bible Expositional Church fulfills the prescriptive command of Paul, "Preach the word" (2 Tim. 4:2). The Jerusalem church is described, "They continued steadfastly in the apostles' teaching" (Acts 2:42).

The Renewal Church takes as prescriptive direction, "Tarry . . . until ye be endued with power from on high" (Luke 24:49, KJV). What results is the theological description of revival: "Times of refreshing may come from the presence of the Lord" (Acts 3:19).

The Body Life Church fulfills the prescriptive command of "the body edifying itself," as Paul said: "The whole body joined and knit together by what every joint supplieth, according to the effective working by which every part does its share . . . for the edifying of itself in love" (Eph. 4:16).

The Liturgical Church eagerly carries out Jesus' admonition, "The Father seeketh such to worship him" (John 4:23). The elders at Ephesus were described "as they ministered [leitourgikus; i.e., give worship to God] to the Lord" (Acts 13:2).

The Congregational Church is the prescriptive ministry of God's people: "As my Father hath sent me, even so send I you" (John 20:21, KJV). Paul descriptively reflects this view, writing, "You are the body of Christ, and members individually" (1 Cor. 12:27).

Why Now?

These six styles of worship, or philosophies of ministries, seem to have come to the surface since about 1945. These worship styles were not apparent in Victorian England, Colonial America, or even before World War II. Although the biblical functions have been operative since Pentecost, there has not been a gathering of an unique biblical function in many individual churches. The influence of American Christianity as reflected in these six church paradigms was not evident in churches or groups of churches outside our borders. All six qualities have been embryonic in every true church since Pentecost, but it seems now that certain churches or groups of churches are characterized by a dominant trait or style and that this strength has become the adhesive (glue) around which people gather. So why have these dominant worship types manifested themselves now in certain churches and in certain new denominations?

The Interstate and the Internet

The answer lies in the impact of two explosive forces that have shaped our society in the past fifty years. These two formative factors have done to culture in general what they have done to the churches—shaped them into six groups. These two factors are (1) the interstate freeway and (2) the Internet via the computer.

The interstate highway system is a massive transportation link that joined the two coasts of America, crisscrossing every state, making almost every destination available to everyone. Simply stated, the interstate highway represents the explosion of transportation since World War II.

So now people will travel as far to church as they travel to their places of employment or their favorite shops. They travel thirty miles to church and never think of the distance because church is only thirty minutes away. Whereas, the colonial farmer may have traveled one hour by wagon to get to a church that was geographically many miles closer.

The Internet stands for the communication age. It reflects the explosion of modern communication by way of computers, fax, cellular phones and so forth. Internet stands for information access; thus, people have access to almost any fact in our information processing age. Churches tell their story on cable television and local radio, in church newsletters and metro newspapers, on billboards, and by various other inventive means. Everyone seems to know about the different kinds of worship in churches in their community, because they see people worshiping like this on television. Then they decide to drive thirty miles to experience it firsthand. They like what they experience and come back every Sunday.

People know (Internet) and people go (interstate). A retired man and woman used to drive 150 miles every Sunday to my church. I asked them why they came so far. The wife said, "When you get over seventy years old and nothing else in life matters, why not go 150 miles to a church you like because your church is the high point of the week?" When her husband died, she moved into a retirement home near our church so a van could bring her each week.

Obviously, they never came back for Sunday evening services or Wednesday prayer meetings when they lived so far away. But their reasoning is hard to refute. Why not do what you enjoy in life? Since Americans have the money to travel, accessible freeways, and they know what is happening in different churches, why not attend one where they'll get the most out of its worship style?

Spiritual Motives

In addition to the interstate and Internet, there are spiritual factors behind the emergence of these six worship and ministry styles. In the past three decades we have witnessed an explosion of interest in spiritual gifts. At first the curiosity was about tongues. Everyone seemed to be asking, "Do you or don't you speak in tongues?"

While tongues do not seem to be as prominent now as they were in the seventies, the interest in spiritual gifts is still with us. The present drive to study gifts comes from the average Christian who wants to know "What is my gift?" and "How can I serve God with my gift?"

Each of these six styles of worship has a dominant manifestation of a different serving gift. This means that a specific spiritual gift is the glue that holds the worship and ministry together. The Bible Expositional Church is driven by the spiritual gift of teaching. Many pastors of Bible expositional churches sign their letters "Pastor-Teacher." The Evangelistic Church is driven by a pastor who has the spiritual gift of evangelism.

Gift Colonization

In fact, these six styles tend to be colonies of like-gifted parishioners, a situation that has been called "gift colonization." People with a dominant spiritual gift choose a church where their personal dominant gift is also the dominant corporate gift. That's why they feel comfortable in a particular style of worship. They are around people like themselves. This is not a selfish desire to avoid people who are different or who may make them feel uncomfortable. People just naturally sort themselves out in life by arranging to spend time with those who make them feel good and help them accomplish their goals. People feel free to worship with others if they are comfortable with them.

True, the church is a hospital where sinners come for help. But the church is also an island among the terrifying tides of life, a haven where believers can escape for safety and solitude. Churches turn out to be different from each other because of this "gift colonization."

Gift Gravitation

How did "gift colonization" happen? It came about by "gift gravitation." Many don't have a rational reason why they choose a renewal church or a liturgical church. They just know what makes them feel comfortable. The need to exercise their own spiritual gift creates pressure—a kind of internal disequilibrium, driving them toward the church where their gift is honored and exercised by others and where they are appreciated for exercising their gift. This internal pressure is called "gift gravitation."

Gift Assimilation

The final factor explaining the current emergence of the six types of churches is "gift assimilation." Christians choose a church worship style, but may not be able to explain why. A person enjoys the excitement of the Evangelistic Church. They begin attending and eventually join the church even though they don't have the spiritual gift of evangelism. But that gift begins to grow (1 Cor. 12:31; Rom. 1:11; 1 Tim. 4:14; 2 Tim. 1:6). The sermons on soul-winning build a desire to witness to nonbelievers. The example of people going to the altar to accept Christ adds to their personal desire. Perhaps the person takes a course on personal evangelism. All these experiences create a spiritual ability to win souls to Christ. Their spiritual giftedness of evangelism grows.

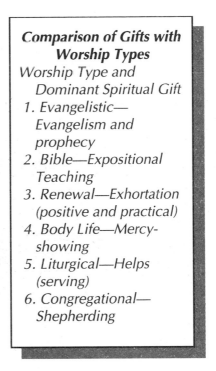

Comparison of Gifts with Worship Types
Worship Type and
   Dominant Spiritual Gift
1. Evangelistic—
   Evangelism and
   prophecy
2. Bible—Expositional
   Teaching
3. Renewal—Exhortation
   (positive and practical)
4. Body Life—Mercy-
   showing
5. Liturgical—Helps
   (serving)
6. Congregational—
   Shepherding

Summary

This book is about North American worship. It is not a description of what is happening around the world. Because worship is an expression of the heart of individuals and the corporate expression of the church body, and because America has a different culture than other countries, we would expect Americans to express their worship differently—in different types of buildings, with different musical instruments, in different languages and dialects.

This book is about America now, not our past. It's not a historical study, and it's not a book on methodology (how to conduct worship).

I do not approve of everything I describe in this chapter. I don't like the consumerism of the world and its influence on the church. Some of you don't like it either. The world does not have the culture we grew up expecting, and the church is not the church for which many of you were trained.

So, let's learn what we need to know about culture. Let's make sure our principles are grounded in the Word of God. Let's make sure we understand what the Bible teaches about worship, and let us communicate that truth to others. But above all else, let's make sure we worship the Father in spirit and in truth.

CHAPTER TWO

My Pilgrimage of Worship

It is not *how* you worship.
It is *who* you worship.

I grew up in the Eastern Heights Presbyterian Church, Savannah, Georgia, enrolling in Sunday school when I was six years old. I never missed one Sunday for fourteen years. I credit my perfect attendance to the character of my mother, who was reared on a farm. She wanted me to grow up to be a man of character, to do the right things in the right way for the right purpose all the time.

I liked going to Sunday school, and a few times I had to stay for the worship service. I didn't particularly enjoy it because I didn't understand what was going on. Some might describe the worship at Eastern Heights Presbyterian Church as liturgical. It was a small congregation of about seventy-five people, and it was not quite as liturgical or formal as a Lutheran or Episcopal service.

In that little Presbyterian church we would follow the order of worship, standing at the appropriate times to sing the Doxology or Gloria Patri. When the pastor asked, "Christian, what do you believe?" I would spring to my feet with the rest of the congregation. I could say perfectly with passion the Apostles' Creed: "I believe in God the Father, Almighty, Maker of heaven and earth, and in Jesus Christ, His only Son . . ." and so forth.

Because I didn't understand most of the worship service, it was boring to me as a child. The hymns were heavy and the moanful "Amen" at the end of each hymn seemed anticlimactic. I liked the peppy songs we sang in Sunday school.

When I was old enough, I started riding my bicycle to church. On the way home, I would pass empty fields and would roll back my head and sing at the top of my voice the concluding "Amen" refrain, "A-a-a-a-m-m-m-m-e-e-e-e-n-n-n-n." While it was not the intent of my heart, I was probably blaspheming the good intent of the message of the great hymns of the past. However, now that I have been converted and now understand the meaning of these great hymns, I keep a hymnbook on my desk and sing them during my morning private devotions. I especially love to sing the hymns that end in "Amen," for these hymns are prayers to God. These great hymns pour out worship to God, and it is fitting that they end in "Amen." I've asked God to forgive the intent of my youthful heart and to make the prayer that ends each of these hymns the intent of my heart.

I was saved in an "atmospheric revival" when two young Bible college students came to pastor the Bonna Bella Presbyterian Church in Savannah, Georgia, bringing renewal to our little fishing village. During an evangelistic crusade, many young people from my church were converted in this little church. The singing was loud and from the heart. I liked that. Young girls sang solos passionately from the heart. I liked that. The two Bible college students preached evangelistically, which means they preached with passion, enthusiasm, and feeling. I liked that. Every night people went to the altar and knelt to be saved. I liked that.

The type of preaching where I was saved is the type of preaching I developed in Bible college. I preached my first sermon on the street corners of Columbia, South Carolina. It was a passionate sermon with lots of fire but little substance beyond the elementary contents of the plan of salvation.

How My Preaching Developed

When I was nineteen years old and a second-year student at Columbia Bible College, I became part-time pastor of the Westminster Presbyterian Church, Savannah, Georgia. Part of my job expectation, and in return for a small salary of five dollars per week, was typing out the church bulletin and mimeographing it each week. The church bought a mimeograph machine, and for awhile I kept it in my father's garage. The church service that I conducted was a strange mixture. The first half of the worship service included the traditional Presbyterian liturgy. In the second half I preached like a revivalist at camp meeting. Since I had been converted in an atmospheric revival, I felt that I had to preach enthusiastically, with emotion, driving home my message. I always ended my sermon with an invitation—an altar call—for people to come forward and kneel, where we would lead them to Christ. In terms of worship expressions, my first pastorate was a liturgical church for the first half of the service and a combination of a renewal church and evangelistic church for the second half.

I remember one of the teenagers at the Presbyterian church asking, "Why do we do all that junk in the beginning?" I knew what he meant. We stood for Responsive Reading, the Apostles' Creed, the Gloria Patri, and all other expressions of liturgy. This teenager went on to say, "I just like it when you rear back and preach."

I was so young in my first church that the people didn't feel comfortable calling me Pastor or Minister. I was not ordained, so they couldn't call me Reverend. Because I loved to preach with passion and motivate them to make a decision at the altar, everyone in the community called me "Preacher."

Next I moved to Dallas, Texas, to attend Dallas Theological Seminary. My wife and I attended two or three Presbyterian churches looking for a church home. Since I had already been a student pastor of Westminster Presbyterian Church, I was looking for a place of service, also an evangelistic Presbyterian church in which I would feel comfortable.

About the fourth week in Dallas, my wife and I attended First Baptist Church, where Dr. W. A. Criswell was pastor. That Sunday night my wife woke up with excruciating pain and was taken to the Baylor Hospital for an emergency surgery to save her life. When the nurse was filling out the admittance papers, she asked for our church home.

"We don't have one," I replied.

She asked what church we had attended that day. I told her First Baptist Church, and I didn't think anything about it.

When I entered the postsurgery ward to see my wife, Dr. Schaffer, the visitation pastor from First Baptist Church, was with my wife. He was an elderly man with angel-white hair.

"I know you kids don't have any money, so the church will help you out," he said.

That night when I got home, the young adult Sunday school teacher from First Baptist Church and his wife were waiting outside with a casserole for my dinner. She went in, cleaned the house, and washed the dishes before leaving. He told me that someone from the Sunday school class would be there every evening with dinner. I told my wife, "First Baptist

Church is a great church. Let's attend this church to learn why it is great." Since I was going into the Presbyterian ministry, I felt I could learn much about ministry from this church. Then I said to her, "But let's not become Baptists."

For his first thirteen years in this church, Dr. Criswell preached from Genesis 1:1 to Revelation 22:21. My wife and I attended the church from Romans 4 to 1 Corinthians 1.

Under the preaching of Dr. Criswell, I changed my theological view of baptism from sprinkling to immersion. Dr. Criswell told the details of this story in the introduction to my book *Sunday School Encyclopedia* (Wheaton: Tyndale, 1991), but my change was more than a change in the mode of baptism. I was giving up reformed theology and becoming a dispensationalist. To be a dispensationalist means that I believed God dealt with people differently in the church dispensation than He did under Law. Since the church is a baptized body of local believers with a different dynamic that held people together than in the Old Testament, it meant the New Testament church was different in function from the Old Testament temple worship. Baptist worship is built on the dynamics of the church in the Book of Acts. Liturgical worship was built on the majesty of the Old Testament temple worship. There is truth in both, but there is also difference in focus. My experience at First Baptist Church was comfortable. It reminded me of the little Bonna Belle Presbyterian Church where I was saved. It was an evangelistic church. Dr. Criswell preached the way I wanted to preach, with dignity and soul-winning fervency.

I attended Dallas Theological Seminary for four years, majoring in systematic theology. Its view of preaching and ministering began to change the way I preached. As I looked at my old sermons, I was embarrassed because there was so little Bible in them. When I preached revivalistically, I read the Bible as the basis of my sermons, told stories to move my listeners emotionally, and gave an invitation to get a decision of their will.

Dallas taught me to preach differently. Dr. Lewis Sperry Chafer, the seminary founder, said, "You haven't preached the gospel until you have given people something to believe." I learned Greek and Hebrew and how to exegete the meaning of text in the original language. I learned to "get my listeners into the Word, and get the Word into my listeners."

During my last two years at Dallas Seminary, I pastored Faith Bible Church, and my preaching vacillated between revivalistic preaching and

Bible expositional preaching, depending on whether I wanted to move the congregation or if I wanted to inform them.

After graduating I became a professor at Midwest Bible College, Saint Louis, Missouri. I was comfortable with my preaching. I still had a passion for evangelistic preaching, whether revivalistic or just plain soul-winning. But also, I still had a warm place in my heart for the dignity of liturgical worship as found in my Presbyterian roots.

At Midwest Bible College, many of the students were from Brethren Assemblies, commonly called Plymouth Brethren Assemblies. I was invited to speak in many of their assemblies, at least the open assemblies. I brought the warmth of evangelistic preaching, tied to Bible exposition from my Dallas Seminary training. In the Brethren Assemblies I began to taste the reality of what later I would call "body life worship." I realized there was biblical reality as people related to one another in honest simplicity. The honesty at the Lord's Table revealed to me two spiritual realities that I had not yet experienced: (1) the power of the laity in worship and service; (2) people find the meaning of their life in honest relationship one to another.

Another experience in Saint Louis changed my perspective on worship. During the summer of 1960, I was hired at $100 a week as executive secretary of the Greater Saint Louis Sunday School Association. The organization was making plans to host the National Sunday School Convention to be held in October of that year in Saint Louis. I visited most of the churches belonging to the association to rally support for the convention, as well as many Assemblies of God, Churches of God, Pentecostal Holiness churches, and Independent Pentecostal churches. Because of my dispensational background, I had deep questions about the movement; I even questioned whether some even knew the Lord. But I found my Pentecostal friends to have great dignity, warmth of passion for Christ, commitment to holiness, and love of brotherhood. My assumptions about "wildfire" in their services were proven wrong. Many of their worship services were like Baptist services, and some churches even had liturgy like Presbyterians or Methodists. From that day forward, I became a friend of Pentecostals, and they became my friends.

In 1969 I published the book *The Ten Largest Sunday Schools and What Made Them Grow* (Grand Rapids: Baker Book House). C. Peter Wagner of Fuller Theological Seminary calls this the first American church growth book and the first book focusing on the megachurch movement. What made this book unique was that I formed a data pool of ten churches—that is, ten case studies from which I drew conclusions. Church Growth is a discipline that is committed to a study of the planting, growth, and death of churches with a view of establishing growth principles. In this book I established many principles by which these ten churches grew. According to Robert Walker, editor of *Christian Life,* it "hit the evangelical world like a thunderclap." In a day when everyone thought the church should be small and mass media thought the church was dying, *The Ten Largest Sunday Schools* demonstrated that churches were alive and well in heartland America.

Classifying the Different Worship Styles

Previously, I had worshiped God in several ways. I knew there was a difference between the Evangelistic Church, the Liturgical Church, the Bible Expositional Church, and the Body Life Church I experienced among the Plymouth Brethren in Saint Louis. Even though I experienced these in my heart and had these church types in my head, I had not yet classified them.

When I studied the ten largest churches, I described each church as an evangelistic church. I assumed that a church had to be an evangelistic church to be a growing church. While that was an early assumption of mine, I slowly changed my mind.

And how did my mind change? During the seventies, John Vaughan and I were preparing a manuscript (along with David Seifert) that was later called *The Complete Book of Church Growth* (Wheaton, Ill.: Tyndale House, 1979). Our intent was to write a book that would be a complete list of all of the principles that would grow a church. The only problem as we began to write out our principles was we faced data that was confusing to us.

We found Bible expositional churches that were growing, yet didn't have soul-winning visitation, altar calls, Sunday school bus visitation, or any of the other principles that we saw in the growing evangelistic churches. So we decided there were two different types of church growth: (1) the Evangelistic Church growth principles and (2) the Bible Expositional Church growth principles that were evident in men like John MacArthur, Chuck Swindoll, and later in Bible teachers such as Charles Stanley.

At first John Vaughan and I thought Pentecostal churches grew when they became evangelistic churches, like Independent Baptist or Southern Baptist. We felt a Pentecostal church had to be committed to soul-winning to grow. But our research revealed churches that were growing because of renewal, revival, and excitement. We began by giving this the title Charismatic Renewal. Then we began to find Southern Baptist churches, independent churches, and other denominational churches that embraced renewal worship services but were not charismatic in theology or practice.

We finally concluded that there were six types of worship services. Originally, we gave the six types of worship services titles that were theological or prescriptive in nature. These titles were printed in the *Complete Book of Church Growth.*

1. Fundamentalism

2. Body Life

3. Charismatic Renewal

4. Evangelical Bible Churches

5. Southern Baptist

6. Mainline Denominations

These titles were too theological and denominational in focus. We needed to make them more descriptive of what they did in evangelism and worship. There were many churches that followed the Southern Baptist approach but did not belong to the Southern Baptist Convention.

Then we found all six worship styles among Southern Baptist churches. Also, we found that the theological titles became barriers to people. Therefore with time, the titles changed.

1. Evangelistic Church

2. Body Life remained the same

3. Renewal Church

4. Bible Expositional Church

5. Congregational Church

6. Liturgical Church

Obviously, Fundamentalism reflected a certain theological stance, whereas the Evangelistic Church reflected those congregations that focused on soul-winning and outreach. At the same time, I found many churches fundamental in position that were not evangelistic in nature, and many churches of other theological persuasion that were in fact evangelistic.

Several Southern Baptist pastors in Baton Rouge, Louisiana, were getting pressure from denominational officials about their worship style. They had a praise band, congregants lifted their hands in worship, and they had done away with the choir, the traditional pulpit, and the traditional organ. Because they were in the area where Jimmy Swaggart, a charismatic, was located, they were accused of becoming charismatic. But these Southern Baptist pastors had not changed their theology, only their worship methodology. As a result of this confusion, I no longer called this worship style Charismatic Renewal, because many churches that were not charismatic in theological expression were in fact renewal in worship style.

I also had to change the name from Evangelical Bible Church to Bible Expositional Church. When the term *evangelical* is used, it identifies a certain theology that is usually associated with the National Association of Evangelicals in Wheaton, Illinois. But I found certain churches that were not theologically aligned with evangelicals, yet they were Bible expositional churches. So the name was changed to the descriptive title, the Bible Expositional Church, which reflected its form of pulpit communication.

The title Southern Baptist was changed to the Congregational Church. I found not all Southern Baptist churches followed a congregational worship format. Some are liturgical, while others like Charles Stanley's have a Bible expositional ministry. Also, many churches not belonging to the Southern Baptist denomination in fact reflect their type of governments and worship. Therefore, the name was changed to Congregational Church to reflect these churches' methodology.

The title Mainline Churches was changed to Liturgical Churches, which reflects a God-centered type of worship. Whereas many of the mainline churches are liturgical in worship, this title identified denominational lines, not worship methodology.

Three Questions

Today, when I teach the six expressions of worship to my students at Liberty Baptist Theological Seminary (or other seminaries where I teach), I always ask the students three questions.

1. *What was the type of worship in the church where you were converted?* Then I explain to the students that they will have certain assumptions about worship that they have assimilated nonverbally. As a result, people who have been converted in an informal setting usually have a difficult time gravitating to a formal liturgical worship service. Sometimes, people are critical of formal worship services for no other reason than the way they were nurtured spiritually. They don't like it because they do not understand it.

2. *What is the type of worship in the church where you now attend?* I want them to understand some of the reasons for the tensions they may have with their present church. Because attitudes are picked up nonverbally, people may have an allegiance to a certain church worship type because they were converted in that type of church worship. When people understand the reasons for their feelings, they can better deal with them.

3. *What kind of worship service will you lead when you become a pastor?* With this third question, I deal with their dreams and aspirations. I want the pastors to articulate their inner desires.

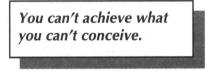

You can't achieve what you can't conceive.

If I can help my students understand the type of worship service that lies in their subconscious, they will have a much better chance of building that type of worship service in the future.

Now that I have taken my pilgrimage in life, and I have an understanding of the different contributions of each worship expression, where do I find myself?

I presently worship in an evangelistic church, the Thomas Road Baptist Church, Lynchburg, Virginia. Everything in the worship service focuses toward the gospel invitation given at the end of each sermon, when many times we sing "Just As I Am." Unsaved people are invited to walk forward and meet a counselor where "you will be taken to a counseling room by a trained worker who will answer your questions and help you to pray to receive Christ." I am very comfortable in this type of service, and I usually am one of the counselors at the altar. Sometimes I kneel with people at the altar, where they pray to receive Christ. Sometimes I take them to the counseling room, where I try to answer their questions or solve other types of problems. I enjoy working with a pastor who has a strong spiritual gift of evangelism, and I am fulfilled ministering in a church that is winning people to Christ.

I am a graduate of Dallas Theological Seminary, and I want to believe I have a high regard for the Bible expositional preaching of the Word of God. I have a deep commitment to the Word of God as the instrument of regeneration. When people understand the Scriptures, they are born again by the Word of God. I recognize that Bible expositional churches are most effective among a clientele of people who are reached by rational questions, pursuit of knowledge, and are motivated by rationality and understanding.

Because I was saved in an atmospheric revival, I still love the Renewal Church, and I love revivalistic preaching. While I tend not to respond as emotionally as others, I still love it. I do not want to pour other people into my test tube and make them fit my formula. I define revival as "God pouring His presence on His people." I want to be there when revival happens.

The Body Life Church is definitely a biblical expression of *koinonia,* the fellowship of believers. Dale Galloway explained his New Life Community Church of Portland, Oregon: "My church doesn't have cells, my church is cells." By that he indicated that the relationship of people one to another in small groups and their spiritual care for one another was the core of all that his church had become. In a world of anonymity and impersonalizations, the Body Life Church meets the crying need of individuals who feel like lost twigs floating down the current of life with no purpose.

I was raised Presbyterian, and I didn't always appreciate the depth of worship that was offered. Now, I love going into what they call the "sanctuary" and listening to a pastor pray the "invocation," where he invites the very presence of God to enter that building and envelope all the believers there. Liturgy has mystery, and exposure to the "wholly other One." I am strengthened in the sacred moments of witnessing my faith by repeating the Apostles' Creed or singing, "Holy, holy, holy, Lord, God Almighty." In these moments I lift my soul up to God in heaven and worship Him. Then I realize that my singing has been a prayer, so I reverently conclude the hymn with the musical benediction "Amen."

I am a Baptist, and I appreciate the simplicity of the Congregational Church. The people are the body of Christ, and He indwells each believer, as they have been placed positionally in Him. The building is not a sacred place of geography, but the room becomes holy as Christ in each believer is magnified. When each believer joins heart with another believer, together they worship God by singing, "What a wonderful change in my life has been wrought, since Jesus came into my heart." In a congregational church the worship service belongs to the people, not to the great Bible teacher, the soul-winning evangelist, or even to the one leading liturgy. It is the people's church, and they are exhorted to love, obey, and worship.

Summary

I respect all forms of worship for the strength I find in each. Obviously, there are some of all styles in each church, but the church that becomes all things to all men makes no contribution to any. But remember, the church is the body of Jesus Christ on this earth. The most important factor of a church is not its name, nor its unique theological stance, nor its worship style. The most important thing about a church is Jesus Christ, meeting Him, learning Him, feeling Him, yielding to Him, and leaving church to serve Him.

CHAPTER THREE

Researching Worship Differences

In worship we see the unseeable, we hear the unhearable, and experience the untouchable.

Worship is the bridge between heaven and earth. Jesus asked Nicodemus, "If I have told you earthly things and you do not believe, how will you believe if I tell you heavenly things?"

(John 3:12)

I have suggested that everyone must worship God because we are commanded to worship God. At the same time I have suggested people worship God differently. This chapter discusses the basics for the various ways of expressing our worship of God. But even as we look at the differences among worshipers, let us not forget the unifying core of all New Testament worship: God.

This section will focus on three discussions. First, we worship differently because of cultural differences. God made ethnic-linguistic people groups differently, and they retain their unique language and identity. Even though each group of people join the rest of the body of Christ to worship God, each group will do it a little differently because true worship must come from our innermost being.

Second, we worship differently because we have different spiritual gifts. The ministry of each spiritual gift will develop a response in believers that reflects that gift. But that response will be different from others with different gifts. We are different people, but united in the one body of Christ. Our differences contribute to the glory of God when we worship from the strength of who we are.

Third, we worship differently because we understand the commands and principles of Scripture differently and apply them differently. The developing discipline of Church Growth is built on identifying and teaching the principles of reaching lost people with the gospel and building them up in their faith.[1] This discipline makes a distinction between universal principles (we must worship God) and methods (how to worship God). A proper understanding of this discipline will help you understand why people worship differently and why God accepts each person who worships God with integrity, based on biblical principles.

God Loves All Peoples

The Christian does not believe that the differences between races and ethnic-linguistic people groups came from evolution. Paul established two truths in his sermon on Mars Hill: (1) God created all people of one blood (i.e., "We be brethren," Gen. 13:8) and (2) "Our differences of race come from God."

"[God] himself gives all men life and breath and everything else. From one man he made every nation *[ethnos]* of men, that they should inhabit the whole earth; and he determined the times set for them and the exact places where they should live" (Acts 17:25–26, NIV). Because God made all people from Adam, we are human beings, indwelt with intellect, emotion, and will; everyone is made in the image of God. God is also the source of our unique differences: different colors, different languages, and different places of origin. Because of our unity in one blood, God loves us equally; and in our differences, God loves us equally.

Into a world of different people groups (sometimes called tribes, nations, minorities, countries, races, Gentiles, heathen, classes, ethnic groups, etc.), God sent His Son to love the world (John 3:16), die for the world (John 1:29), and have a plan for the world (Luke 21:24).

Jesus commanded His disciples, "Go ye into all the world, and preach the gospel to every creature" (Mark 16:15, KJV). This command was to go and preach to every person. He described the world as a single unit and each person as an individual. That is the Lord's focus in Mark. But one aspect was left out of this command. Later, Jesus added the aspects of ethnic-linguistic people groups: "Go therefore and make disciples of all nations *[ethne],* baptizing them in the name of the Father and of the Son and of the Holy Spirit, teaching them to observe all things that I have commanded you" (Matt. 28:19–20).

Jesus did not tell His disciples to just preach to people groups (*ethne*), but to make disciples of them.[2] He no longer talked about the world as a unit. He commanded them to reach people in the culture where they lived. Jesus meant we must reach across linguistic, ethnic, and class barriers to bring people to Himself, then build churches in each linguistic, ethnic, and class group to help each person grow in Christ.[3]

In our modern society, racism has become a distinct problem, and at the root of the problem of racism is sin. A believer should look beyond the sin of racism to see that:

- God has created all peoples: "From one man he made every nation *[ethne]* of men, that they should inhabit the whole earth" (Acts 17:26, NIV);
- God has planned that each *ethne* would be a continuing homogeneous unit: "He determined the times set for them and the exact places where they should live" (Acts 17:26, NIV);
- The peoples should have the gospel presented to them (Matt. 28:19–20);
- Each people group should have disciples following Jesus according to the customs and values of that people (baptize them and teach them);
- Each nation must be evangelized, "So that all nations *[ethne]* might believe and obey Him" (Rom. 16:26, NIV);
- Representatives from all peoples would remain unique as they worship God in heaven: "After this I looked and there before me was a great multitude that no man could count, from every nation, tribe, people and language, standing before the throne . . . wearing white robes. . . . And they cried out in a loud voice: 'Salvation belongs to our God, who sits on the throne, and to the Lamb'" (Rev. 7:9–10, NIV).

To carry out the command of reaching all nations, we must recognize certain Church Growth principles, such as the homogeneous unit principle.[4] This principle recognizes the inclusive nature of each people group as reflected in its values, attitudes, and perspectives. It also recognizes that they are different in culture from others but that each individual from each people group retains the humanness of all people. This is true because they are made in the image of God: "God, who made the world and everything in it . . . gives to all life, breath, and all things" (Acts 17:24–25).

With the recognition of differences between groups, we must also recognize that there are barriers to reaching people for Christ, from one group to another.[5] We cannot assume that the values of American culture or

Christianity will be accepted in a different culture; rather, the values, attitudes, and culture of American society may in fact be a hindrance to the communication of the gospel to a different culture. For example, different cultures place different values on musical instruments. Children prize the sounds they heard growing up. It is the gospel sung in the music of their hearts that will call them to God. Music that is strange to the ear will be a barrier to reaching them with salvation.

Worship will follow the same cultural expression. The musical instruments of a culture will reach people in that culture better than an instrument that is foreign. By using the European organ in foreign cultures, we are attempting to "Westernize" them before "Christianizing" them.

We must understand culture to understand worship. This does not mean we adapt the gospel to their culture. The gospel never changes, and the message never changes. People must worship from the depths of their heart—that's the place where the difference lies. But what is in the heart? Because different cultures value different items with their heart, it is the heart expression that's different from one culture to another. So the worshiper must be born again by the blood of Christ. The object of worship must be the Father. But each culture will use different language, musical instruments, and expressions in its worship. Each will worship differently according to the emotions of its people's hearts.

Differences of Spiritual Gifts

Every believer is gifted with spiritual gifts, yet each person is different from others. "Each one has his own gift from God, one in this manner and another in that" (1 Cor. 7:7).

The sovereignty of God is behind the differences of spiritual gifts. Paul notes the way God gives different gifts. "There are different kinds of gifts, but the same spirit. There are different kinds of service, but the same Lord. There are different kinds of working, but the same God works all of them in all men" (1 Cor. 12:4–6, NIV).

There are six expressions of worship and each worship expression tends to reflect a dominant spiritual gift.[6] A spiritual gift is a God-given ability to perform spiritual ministry to God. When a church has many people with the same dominant spiritual gift, then the worship and ministry of that congregation is controlled by those who express that gift.

- The Evangelistic Church—Gift of Evangelism
- The Bible Expositional Church—Gift of Teaching

- The Renewal Church—Gift of Exhortation
- The Body Life Church—Gift of Mercy-Showing
- The Liturgical Church—Gift of Helps/Ministry
- The Congregational Church—Gift of Administration

In each of these six expressions the Bible is used. Obviously, in the Evangelistic Church the Bible is used overtly in gospel songs, testimonies, Scripture reading, and the sermon to bring people to Jesus Christ. In the Bible Exposition Church, the Bible is usually taught for full understanding. But even when the focus of the sermon is not specifically evangelistic, the unsaved person may be convicted of sin. In the Renewal Church, unsaved people experience the Bible as it is used in praise music, testimonies, sermons, and worship of God. Hence, people may get saved in renewal churches even though the specific purpose is not evangelistic preaching. In Body Life churches, the Bible becomes the basis of relationship and fellowship from one believer to another. The Bible is shared, taught, and becomes the basis of sermons, music, and testimony. As a result of preaching the Bible in Body Life churches, people are brought to Jesus Christ. The Liturgical Church is filled with the Bible, however the service technically does not have any evangelistic thrust. The Bible is evident in hymns, scriptural reading, the Apostles' Creed, and the reading of liturgy, whether Lutheran, Episcopal, Presbyterian, or high church Methodist. In the Congregational Church, the Bible becomes the basis for all ministry by and for the people of God. They sing the words of Scripture, give reverence for holy living, testify, and preach the Bible.

Any one of the six expressions is not more biblical than the other, each one carries out its own function, and each can bring the unsaved to a saving knowledge of Jesus Christ. Whereas the Evangelistic Church is more outwardly committed to the process of soul-winning, evangelism does take place in each of the other expressions of worship.

In the process of bringing believers to maturity, each worship expression makes its contribution. Obviously, the Bible Expositional Church is committed to the process of building up believers by teaching the Word of God to them in obedience to the command: "Grow in the grace and knowledge of our Lord and Savior Jesus Christ" (2 Pet. 3:18). But the Renewal Church is also committed to maturity when it seeks to stir each believer to a daily renewed commitment to Jesus Christ. The Body Life Church is committed to the growth of believers through fellowship, support, and encouragement of one with another. "The whole body, joined and held together by every supporting ligament [of the believers], grows and builds itself up" (Eph. 4:18, NIV). The Liturgical Church brings believers to maturity as each one worships God, "Let everything that has breath praise the LORD" (Ps. 150:6). And as believers lift up the Lord in their life, they grow, thereby becoming a better disciple of Jesus Christ. The Congregational Church focuses on the involvement of every believer, "Just as you received Christ Jesus as Lord, continue to live in him, rooted and built up in him, strengthened in the faith as you were taught, and overflowing with thankfulness" (Col. 2:6–7, NIV).

The church has its existence apart from believers, but is made up of many believers, each of them different. "The body is a unit, though it is made up of many parts; and though all its parts are many, they form one body" (1 Cor. 12:12, NIV). Just as each Christian has his unique spiritual gift, calling, and cultural background, so each local church is an expression of the total gifts in that body. "God has arranged the parts in the body, every one of them, just as he wanted them to be" (1 Cor. 12:18, NIV).

Just as God has given some people the gift of evangelism, others are teachers, some have the gift of serving, while others have the gift of showing mercy. Just as Christians are different, so churches are different—each carrying out the unique calling that God has given them. From the reading of the Epistles written to churches (Corinth, Ephesus, Philippi), we see that each church had unique strengths, weaknesses, and passions; however within the Great Commission, the churches had a unity of passion, purpose, and fellowship.

If God has made Christians different, as well as making churches different, who can say that an evangelistic church is better than a worshiping liturgical church? Who can say that a Bible expositional church is better than a congregational church?

Church Growth as a Discipline

The growth in understanding and acceptance of the various expressions of worship has paralleled the development of Church Growth as a discipline. Both of these have emerged into public view since World War II. I do not think there is a cause-effect relationship between the two; it's just that our changing culture has forced the church to apply its ministry to the new innovations of society in which the church ministers. Since both the new expressions of worship and Church Growth have emerged in these explosive times, it means there are correlations, but one is not demanded by the other.

The discipline of Church Growth grew in the heart and mind of Donald McGavran, a missionary to India. McGavran saw the success of some missionaries in evangelizing the unreached with the gospel, but the efforts failed when applied to people of a different caste. McGavran began to realize he needed "cross-cultural evangelism" to reach from one caste to another.[7] Certain castes in India were untouchable, which made preaching the gospel ineffective. The problem was not the gospel message, but the barriers of culture. McGavran came to the conclusion that when the evangelist followed certain laws or principles in doing the work of evangelism, they were successful. He called these principles "cross-cultural evangelism." Since he was concerned with evangelism crossing from one caste to another caste, or "untouchables," he titled his book *The Bridges of God*.[8]

McGavran needed a term to help people understand his new principles.[9] He didn't want to use the term *evangelism* because of its misconceptions: Some thought evangelism was a crusade with a special speaker known as an evangelist; others thought of evangelism as learning a catechism or joining a church through membership; still others in India thought they had to become Westernized to become a Christian. McGavran concluded there was too much baggage with the term *evangelism*, so he looked for another term.

McGavran thought through the process: (1) preach the gospel; (2) they believe; (3) they are baptized and join the church; (4) the church grows. So he concluded, why don't we use the *output* term (church growth) instead of the *input* term (evangelism)?

So the new system of following cross-cultural principles in evangelism was called Church Growth. (He capitalized it because it defined an entity or movement, and was more than a description of something that would use the lower case.)

Three Ideas about Church Growth

1. Numbers. Some think Church Growth is about an increase in numerical figures of a church, such as growth in attendance, offerings, membership, baptisms, etc. Numerical growth is the *result* of Church Growth but is not the dynamic heart that produces growth. A passion for the lost produces growth. Church Growth involves numbers, but more than numbers.

2. Church Planting. At the beginning of the movement many equated Church Growth with church planting. McGavran said the best way to evangelize a caste is not for a foreigner to preach to them. He concluded the best way to reach "untouchables" was to plant a church in their culture and have members of that church who were "untouchable" to evangelize their friends, neighbors, relatives, and associates. Church planting resulted in "untouchables" evangelizing "untouchables."

Church planting in a culture by the people of that culture who govern and support the church in their culture is the biblical principle of evangelism. While church planting is a part of the Church Growth movement, Church Growth is more.

3. A Science. McGavran realized we must follow principles for effective evangelism.[10] At first he began to formulate principles from his observation. When these principles began to crystallize in his thinking, he wrote them down and gave them names or titles, such as the Homogenous Unit, People Movement, and so forth. He recognized it would take certain expressions of evangelism to overcome barriers, so titles were given, such as "E-1," which means "Evangelism to overcome the first barrier"—the church building, church name, or outward expressions of Christianity. Hence, E-1 evangelism overcomes the "stained glass barrier." Obviously, stained glass is not always a barrier to evangelizing people outside the church, but stained glass was a symbolic word that stood for the external factors that hindered evangelism.

E-0 Evangelism of those already in the church

E-1 Stained Glass Barrier: evangelizing those outside the church

E-2 Cultural and Class Barriers: evangelizing those of a different culture

E-3 Linguistic Barriers: evangelizing those of a different language

The term *science* scares some readers, and immediately they think that science has thrown God out the window. But that is not the case; as a matter of fact, the opposite is true. True science will consider all facts, which is another way of saying true science will consider all truth. It must consider the data about God, the Scriptures, the history of Christianity; that is, all truth must be evaluated in arriving at true principle.

The church has faced the problem of ineffective evangelism. It asks questions: What are the barriers to reaching people for Christ? How can the task of evangelism be done more effectively? The science of Church

Growth has gathered data from any and every service. It begins with the Bible to get its mandate and marching orders. The principles of the Bible are analyzed to make sure the church properly understands what God meant. Also, data from culture are examined to determine how best to reach people with the gospel. Facts are gathered from church history, case studies, surveys, and interviews. Church Growth methodology gathers information from any and every source concerning God and His world.

The next step in the scientific methodology is to suggest a solution to the problem. The educational world calls this solution a hypothesis (from Latin, *hypo*; "proposal and thesis, a law or principle to solve a problem"). A hypothesis is a suggested law or an unproven thesis.

Then the hypothesis must be tested to determine if it is true or valid. Since truth is consistent with itself and corresponds with the rest of the world, any new principle

> ### The Scientific Method
> 1. Begin with a problem.
> 2. Gather data/facts to
>   solve the problem.
> 3. Suggest a hypothesis to
>   solve the problem.
> 4. Test the hypothesis to
>   determine its validity.
> 5. Establish a principle(s)
>   to solve the problem.

must be consistent with all other truth and it must fit into the world as we know it is true. Since the Bible is the highest truth, any Church Growth principle must be in harmony with Scripture and correspond to what God is doing in the world.

After a suggested principle is validated, then it is presented to the church. Most Church Growth authorities like to give a name to the principle they discover and verify. *Christianity Today* accused the Church Growth Movement of inventing "cute" and fancy titles for the principles it discovered. McGavran began with the names Homogeneous Unit and People Movement. After I studied the research of Flavil Yeakley, I gave the names "The Law of Three Hearings" and "The Law of Seven Touches" to his results.[11] As I edited *The Practical Encyclopedia of Evangelism and Church Growth,* I discovered the Church Growth leaders had literally hundreds of names for this growing discipline.

Methodology Applied to Worship

How can we determine which worship is best overall? Which worship is best for you? A few church leaders want to control the worship expression of others. They seem to say, "My way of worship is the best way. My way of worship is the only way."

Like a battery with two poles to produce power, there are two factors to make worship valid or authentic. First, worship must be in keeping with the Word of God. God must be worshiped as He is revealed in Scripture—adding nothing to Him, taking nothing from Him. The Bible, and only the Bible, verifies the validity of your worship. Second, you must worship sincerely from your innermost being, with all your heart, with all your soul, and with all your mind (Matt. 22:37).

Applying the research methodology of Church Growth, we begin with a problem. Different cultures use different musical instruments to praise God. Different age groups express their love with different types of music. Different socio-economic classes (upper class and lower class) express their values by different ways of singing. Like the differences among the caste system of India that produce the "untouchable," America has cultural differences. Must all Americans express their worship the same way? What expression of worship is best?

Data must be gathered. This involves looking at the purpose or aim of worship. Next, the principles of worship must be established. Finally, the desired results of worship in the individual must be established. These facts are gathered, analyzed, and classified in chapters 5 through 10.

Next, the hypothesis or proposed solution is suggested. Rather than saying there is only one expression of worship (e.g., the European tradition), this text suggests there are six valid expressions of worship. Each expression reflects a dominant biblical principle, and each produces a biblical result in the life of the worshiper.

The six worship expressions must be tested by Scripture. Do they fit a biblical mode, and does each follow biblical principles? Does each worship expression produce biblical results? When the results are consistent with Scripture and they correspond to Christian tradition and history, then there is credibility in the six worship expressions.

Summary

If there are six valid worship expressions, whereby each born-again believer can worship the one true God with his entire being, then there remains some therapy for the body of Christ. Christians have disagreed, and they have fought. They have destroyed churches, split churches, and quit churches—all over worship. They have ostracized pastors, criticized pastors, and fired pastors—all over worship.

Since worship is the most powerful force exerted by the creature, then it is only natural that it is going to be one of the most difficult energies to harness and direct. Like the enormous danger of atomic nuclear energy, let's pray that worship can be directed for the good of mankind, not its destruction.

CHAPTER FOUR

Worship Wars

The first murder took place between brothers in a disagreement over worship.

The church has had centuries of battles. It has fought theological battles, and those who lost were martyred, such as Servetus, who was burned at the stake by John Calvin. It has had turf wars when denominations fought over the right to evangelize the islands of the South Seas. It has had conquest wars, such as the Crusades to capture Jerusalem. It has had "blood and guts" battles, such as the 1531 battle in which the Christian patriot Ulrich Zwingli died defending the Bible against tradition. The church has fought over doctrine, polity, wicked leaders, corruption, appointing people to positions, and the use of statues in churches.

Today's most agonizing battles are over worship!

Shall We Raise Hands?

A California pastor graduated from a theological seminary where he learned Bible expositional preaching. He spent his life ministering in a church that combined congregational government with Bible expositional preaching. Upon his retirement, the church called a younger pastor who tried to lead the church into renewal worship. A praise band was organized, and praise music was added to the worship service. Since the people liked the preaching of the young pastor, they allowed his "young ways" to attract a younger audience. The young pastor preached on "raised hands" and instructed everyone to lift hands in worship. Two of the pastors on the platform wouldn't follow his instruction. They were older staff members who had served under the former pastor. It was just not in their hearts to do it. One staff member told me he was not being disobedient or rebellious to the new pastor. "I couldn't bring myself to do it," he confessed. "Raising my hands to please the pastor would have been hypocritical because it's not me."

When the older church members saw the division on the platform, they also refused to raise their hands. When the older members began questioning the longtime staff member, he in turn asked, "What shall I do?"

Because of the staff member's integrity, he left the church without causing a ruckus. Many older members who felt uneasy with lifting their hands also left the church.

Casualties: Two staff members lost their positions and older members left the church.

Don't Sit on Your Hands

A church in Tennessee had the opposite result. A young pastor was called to a suburban church because of his enthusiasm. The people liked his energetic preaching and aggressive evangelism. The former pastor was "dead," some said, although he was solid on the fundamentals and he constantly visited in homes, hospitals, and rest homes. The former pastor loved the people. The new pastor attracted young couples who flooded the auditorium. They clapped their hands, shouted "Hallelujah," and pumped the air with their fists. The older folks didn't like applause after special music. The young pastor tried to get everyone to "give a hand to Jesus." The young people responded vigorously. The pastor scolded the older members for "sitting on your hands." At the next board meeting, the members voted unanimously to terminate his services that evening. Even though they paid him for three months in advance and allowed him to stay in the parsonage until they called another pastor, it took him six months to find another church.

Casualties: the pastor's family lost three months' income, and most of the young people, who were recruited by the young pastor, left the church.

From Traditional Church to a Seeker-Driven Church

A large, independent, soul-winning church in Florida was characterized as an evangelistic church. The pastor preached a gospel message Sunday morning, Sunday night, and Wednesday during prayer meeting, followed by an invitation for lost people to walk forward and pray to receive Christ as Savior. The pastor visited a seeker-driven pastor's conference and returned to inaugurate a seeker service in his home church.

The choir and organ were replaced with praise teams and an electronic piano. The hymn books disappeared, and the words to praise music were flashed on a screen. Modern drama was used and announcements were given via large television screens. The invitation was dropped, and members were exhorted to witness to their unchurched friends in the parking lot of the church as they left the services. Sermons were preached in the vernacular from a "user-friendly" point of view. Everything traditional disappeared, and so did people wanting a traditional service. People who left felt abandoned without the music they grew up singing in the church. Most went to a large nearby Southern Baptist church that had a worship service similar to the one previously followed in the independent Baptist church.

Casualties: Approximately one thousand worshipers went elsewhere to worship, and those who stayed had to "downsize" operations because of budget restraints. Several staff positions were dissolved, and the ministers had to seek positions elsewhere.

He Wasn't a Bible Expositor

In 1985 a large East Coast Baptist church was transporting approximately seven hundred bus riders to the Sunday school each Sunday morning. There were about four hundred adults in the worship service. This church fit the Evangelistic Church paradigm, with everything revolving around an aggressive soul-winning program. The pastor who founded the church was frustrated that he couldn't grow the church past 1,100. He began searching for new methods to attract numbers.

The pastor attended a pastor's conference where the workshops instructed him in the methods of a Bible expositional paradigm. The pastor liked the Bible expositional preaching he heard. His sermons back home were shallow at best, so his hungry soul devoured the in-depth sermons.

He returned home to cut back on his bus outreach, canceled Tuesday night evangelistic visitation, and quit giving altar calls at the end of his sermons on Sunday night and at Wednesday prayer meeting. He continued giving an altar call after his Sunday morning sermon. He began preaching verse by verse through Matthew during the next year. Still, he didn't know Hebrew and Greek, and he did not use Bible commentaries. His sermons were still shallow.

He didn't attract new people with his new form of preaching as he expected. He lost some of the old people who didn't like his new preaching style. As the bus routes were cut back, the bus workers left and joined a nearby evangelistic-type church, and their new church sent them into the bus routes of the old neighborhoods. Soon the bus ministry was closed. Since there was no outreach, the pastor stopped giving the altar call on Sunday morning. The church that had averaged 1,100, now averaged a little more than two hundred. Finances became tight, and the facilities became shabby because of deferred maintenance. The pastor was called to a California church seeking a Bible expositional minister.

Casualties: A church lost its neighborhood outreach, a pastor left his church, and bus workers became disillusioned with Bible expositional preaching.

The Gospel Service

A Lutheran church in the Midwest followed the traditional Lutheran liturgy each Sunday. It was classified as a traditional liturgical church. A young pastor brought in what he called a "gospel service" during the Sunday school hour. It was held in the church gym with piano instead of the organ and with gospel songs instead of hymns. It was informal, with testimonies and various laypeople participating in the service. The service in the gym had the blessing of the church board members because they wanted to reach young couples—and this service did it. The service flourished, and the young couples brought their friends from other Lutheran congregations in the metropolitan area.

The pastor was happy, the young couples responded, and the board was pleased until young couples began leaving after the gospel service to go home. Their children had studied the Bible in Sunday school and the young couples had worshiped in the gospel service, so they got on with the activities of the weekend. The board did not consider a gospel service an adequate replacement for the traditional Lutheran liturgy. When they considered dropping the gospel service, several young couples threatened to leave the church and attend a different Lutheran church.

A denominational official was invited to help mediate the impasse. It was decided to offer an early traditional Lutheran liturgy at 8:00 A.M., a gospel service at 9:30 A.M., and another traditional Lutheran liturgy at 11:00 A.M. The board felt "timing" was the problem; they thought the young couples could attend earlier, but most of them didn't. Many of the older Lutherans changed to 8:00 A.M., with only a few of the young people changing services. Today most of the worshipers attend traditional liturgy at 8:00, and a large gospel service is conducted at 9:30. However, over the years it has taken on the characteristics of a seeker service with a praise band, praise musical team, and a drama presentation. The board has accepted the seeker service, but not wholeheartedly.

Casualties: the 11:00 A.M. worship time.

The Platform Church

A Pentecostal church moved from its traditional Sunday morning worship at 11:00 A.M. into a renewal church paradigm. Worship was lengthened from one hour to two, stretching from 10:00 A.M. until noon. Adult Sunday school was shifted to weeknight home cell Bible studies. Attendance jumped forward on Sunday morning, and most of the adults got involved in home Bible studies. True to statistics that reveal the average attender only stays in a cell group twenty-two months, eventually attendance at the weeknight cells began to decline. Something happened to the spirit of the church. Even though the worship services were as lively as ever, the congregation became a "platform church," with little discipleship, lay training, or Bible instruction (the contribution of Sunday school). The church had changed its paradigm from a traditional congregational church to a renewal worship service with a modified body life church. But they didn't make adequate preparations for the shift, and the spiritual health of the church suffered, though its numbers didn't go down.

Casualties: loss of foundational biblical involvement by laypeople in ministry.

Three Attitudes toward Worship

To understand how the areas of tension have changed, refer back to chapter 1 where I indicated that the different paradigms of worship have developed because of the Internet (communication) and the interstate (transportation). Three attitudes toward worship developed after World War II.

Attitude 1: Ignoring Others Because of Ignorance

If anything, most Christians were ignorant of how others worshiped, so they ignored one another. Since the differences in worship had little influence on one another, no one paid much attention to how others did it.

Attitude 2: Attacking Others Because of Threatening Dangers

A few may have attacked one another, but it was probably more because of doctrinal differences than because of worship differences. A fundamentalist, soul-winning church might accuse those with a liturgical lifestyle of having liberal or modernistic theology. Or, the "enthusiast" surely would have attacked the "liturgical" for being "dead" and unappetizing.

Attitude 3: Criticizing Others Because of Irritating Differences

Some might have criticized different worship expressions because of differences in things that surround worship: use of robes and the appearance of the sanctuary. They also criticized the length of sermons, the enthusiasm (or lack of enthusiasm) of preachers, and other things, such as kneelers and stained-glass windows.

Whether people disagreed over doctrine, lifestyle, or even differences in church government, few made worship practice a point of heated controversy.

All this has changed. We now live in a day of doctrinal toleration. Calvinistic Presbyterians are much more tolerant of Arminians than they were in the "good old days." The same can be said for a Wesleyan Methodist being tolerant of a Lutheran. Also, we live in a day of tolerance toward church polity and practice. Everyone knows that the Presbyterian sprinkles babies in a christening service, but seldom do we hear Baptists attacking Presbyterians for their mode of baptism.

"Each generation must fight its own theological battles," observed Charles Ryrie, former professor at Dallas Theological Seminary. He meant that people fighting their theological wars know the differences separating them and realize that they are not going to change one another, so they live at peace with those with a different persuasion. What Ryrie said about differences seems to be true today, except in one area: we seem to live in an era of worship wars.

Theology—Principles—Methods

Worship is the battleground today. Some disagreement may result from theology, but most disagreement is over methods. To understand this difference, the following concentric circles explain the flow from theology to methodology.

Theology is the core, or substance, of truth. The theological beliefs concerning God and His world are our reflections of the true nature of God and how He relates to this world. The truth found in the first circle is called the substance of theology.

Principles express the way God relates to His world or the laws by which He operates His plan and purpose in the world. We speak about the principles of prayer, evangelism, holiness, and training people for a life of godliness. Because principles express truth and the way things operate, principles are transcultural and transtemporal. A principle is always true in every generation for all people of all time.

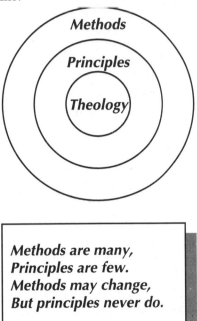

Methods change, though principles remain. They evolve over time and vary from one culture to another. A method is defined as the application of a principle to culture. The Sunday School is the application of the principle of Bible teaching to the culture of the contemporary church. The Sunday School Movement of 1780 did not trace its roots to the New Testament church, though there has been Bible teaching since the New Testament church. But Bible teaching was not organized as we see it taught (i.e., age graded, gender graded, and covering the whole Bible for all the church). The principle of teaching is eternal, but the Sunday School method has been in existence a little more than two hundred years. To

**Methods are many,
Principles are few.
Methods may change,
But principles never do.**

understand the distinction between methods and principles, note the following statement: The differences in worship deal with method, not principle. The principle of singing (Col. 3:16) is a biblical principle, but the method of singing may change from culture to culture. The principle of public prayer is commanded, but the method may be pastoral prayer, lay prayer, concerts of prayer, responsive prayer, or corporately praying the Lord's Prayer.

Some of the tensions mentioned below come from dealing with ethnic matters that change from culture to culture and from time to time. Other tensions deal with matters of principle that involve the very nature of worship. Still other tensions fall in the gray area; we usually have difficulty determining if a tension is substance or application.

Six Areas of Tension

Area 1: Seeker Sensitivity Versus Biblical Values

Certain voices are raising concerns that the seeker-type services have violated the biblical mandate of worship because they target the unsaved rather than the saved. The seeker-driven church (predominantly identified with Bill Hybels and his Willow Creek Community Church in South Barrington, Illinois) is a church that fills a niche by appealing to nonchurch people. The entire church service is planned to present the gospel within the unchurched vocabulary, lifestyle, and social setting.

Bill Hybels and I spoke at a leadership conference held at Skyline Wesleyan Church, Lemon Grove, California, sponsored by Dr. John Maxwell, pastor of the church. In this service, Bill Hybels indicated that he did not have a cross in his church because it offended the unsaved. He felt unbelievers would attend a church building that looked more like a civic center. Hybels claimed when the church looked too liturgical, it raised barriers so the unchurched would not listen to the gospel. He went on to say that he did not want people to lift their hands when they prayed because that makes the unchurched uneasy; for the same reason he didn't want to pray "Our Father who art in Heaven," or sing "This is my Father's world." Hybels uses contemporary drama because the unsaved watch drama on television and it is a vehicle that they understand. Also, he mentioned the music should have the same beat that they hear during the week. Hybels noted that the unsaved do not listen to choirs, organs, and acoustical pianos. They listen to electronic music and small singing groups. They want sermons that help them cope with their problems. Hybels gave prohibitions to follow in reaching the unsaved. The unchurched don't want to:

1. Stand up (to be introduced to the congregation),

2. Sign up (fill out a visitor's card),

3. Speak up (to introduce themselves),

4. Give up (to be asked for money).

There was a day when Bill Hybels did not pass an offering plate because it offended the unsaved. However, today the offering plate is passed with his instructions, "This is only for the member, not for you who are visitors."

The *seeker-driven service* is planned for unchurched or unsaved people. The seeker-sensitive service is similar but has a different thrust. The *seeker-sensitive service* is designed for the Christian, but parts of the program are sensitive to the unchurched. Aspects of the service are interpreted for them.

The seeker-sensitive church is best personified by Rick Warren, Saddleback Church, Mission Viejo, California. At Saddleback Church, drama, singing hymns, and teaching from the Word of God is for the Christian; but it is sensitive to the needs and perspectives of the unchurched visitor as well.

One author who raises major questions about the seeker church is Robert Wenz.[1] He suggests that some churches have gone beyond being sensitive to unbelievers; they have accommodated the unsaved at the cost of violating biblical values.

Some of these criticisms could also be aimed at the southern gospel singing church that uses the same Christian quartet that entertained on Saturday night for the Sunday morning service. Even though these are worship services and the pastor presents an evangelistic message each Sunday morning, there is a great deal of entertainment involved. These southern gospel services appeal to the "blue-collar" crowd rather than the more "white-collar" audience at the seeker-sensitive worship service.

Area 2: Human-Centered Versus God-Centered

Certain critics feel that some churches center too much attention on the "felt needs" of people rather than on God. Obviously, those who hold this criticism have questions about seeker-services, renewal services, or even the body life services. The argument is that those services are planned for people, not for God. Those holding this criticism tend to ask, "What did God get out of the service?" They say that certain churches have stooped to the level of human interest, rather than lifting people up to God's level. They point out that much of today's preaching is functional preaching to help solve the problems of life, rather than emphasizing Bible preaching or liturgical worship.

Why are churches moving toward "felt need" sermons? Because many baby boomers have criticized the church for being unsympathetic to their needs or not being relevant to their problems. As a result, the boomer wants to negotiate a compromise, saying, "If you help me live better Monday through Friday, I will give up my Sunday mornings for your worship service." It's a trade-off. Therefore, boomers are demanding how-to sermons on applied Christianity:

- How to be a better husband
- How to raise children
- How to resolve conflict in your marriage
- How to love deeper
- How to overcome a poor self-image
- How to get more out of your vacation and still be a Christian
- How to make decisions
- What to do when problems come

Those who criticize a practical bent in worship services maintain that when a person meets God, his or her entire life is changed. In the worship experience, the person encounters God and is transformed. The worshiper then comes away with a new orientation of life, new self-worth, new purpose, and a new value. The practical comes after meeting God, not an enticement to get his or her attendance. Dynamic life-changing worship is practical.

The critics claim that the felt-need approach to preaching and worship:

- Fails to take much of its content from the Bible;
- Fails to teach the Bible properly;
- Fails to point people to the life-changing power of God that results in proper discipleship and Spirit-filled living;
- Fails to call worshipers to repentance;
- Fails to develop a spiritual view of the Christian life, instead promoting legalism and works of the flesh.

Area 3: Dumbing Down Rather Than Shaping Up

In her book *Reaching Out Without Dumbing Down*, Marva Dawn, a Lutheran laywoman, argues that contemporary worship forms accommodate the worst in popular culture.[2] They are secular, self-centered, individualistic, and anti-intellectual. Dawn believes that educational standards are being reduced to a lower level in order to accept people where they are rather than lifting people to where they should be. She accuses contemporary worship forms of turning away from the richness of Christianity that brought the church to its greatest height and "dumbing down" to where contemporary people are today. She uses illustrations of the American educational institution that makes tests easier so students can pass, hence bringing school standards down to the level of the student. She indicates that the reading achievement test for ninth graders in 1988 was easier than the one for fourth graders in 1964. As a result, she feels children have learned less than their parents. Some contributing forces to the problem she notes are video games, television, rock videos, and a number of other influences that face today's kids.[3]

Dawn sees a parallel in accommodating culture to contemporary worship just as the church has accommodated culture into contemporary Christian music. With its subtle musical beat, contemporary Christian music gives the young Christians of today what they want, rather than the stimulation they need to lift them to a higher level.[4] Dawn sees the problem as more than a shallow music style; it has become a "slippery slope" that allows contemporary culture and society to tell the church how it wants to worship, when it wants to worship, and what is appropriate for worship. She feels that many churches have made a "devil's pact" with contemporary culture and in the process have stripped themselves of true biblical worship so that the church no longer has the power and influence to change lives that it once had.

Obviously Dawn's problem is more with contemporary culture than it is with the contemporary worship service. She describes contemporary culture as "technological, boomer, post-modern culture."[5] She notes we live in a world that is controlled by television, which makes people passive. She feels television first makes people lose their ability to rationalize; and second, they surrender to the advertising world of marketing and consumerism. The worse thing about the contemporary culture is that it makes individuals lose their individuality, each one conforming to society. As a result, Dawn claims this influence leads to hopelessness, cynicism, and ultimately to humanism and atheism. According to Dawn, "When we 'Dumb Down' the church, then we've prayed to the idolatries of mammon, or power; then we allow our culture sloth or efficiency to control us; then we serve the purposes of evil and allow their principalities and powers to pervert God's designs for believers' character, growth and for their response to God's gift in reaching out to a needy world with the genuine gospel."[6]

Dawn has raised some important points about today's worship, and there are some answers to her attack. She suggests that anything coming from popular culture should be excluded from our worship in the church. She wants us all to retreat into the sanctuary for liturgical worship. But does the worship that she suggests come from a culture that was Christian?

Most advocates of the liturgical worship recognize that it began in Europe and has roots in our Western civilization. Should Asian, Hispanic, African, and Indian cultures follow a Westernized worship? To do that, worship would not come from the heart, but from another culture. In essence, Dawn is asking that we Westernize the world before we Christianize the world. Liturgical worship is a cathedral experience in which the deep tones of European music point us to God. Liturgical worship follows an order of worship that includes such things as the Doxology, the Apostles' Creed, and responsive reading. It comes out of our Western tradition of rationality and lineal thinking. This raises two questions: (1) Is Western culture superior to Asian and African cultures? (2) Must a person become Westernized before becoming Christianized?

Obviously, the answer is that none must be Westernized before they become Christianized. As we examine the Jerusalem Conference (Acts 15), Paul and Silas argued that Gentiles need not become Jews (by circumcision into the Jewish commonwealth) in order to become Christians.

A third question for Dawn is, "Should a church be prevented from adapting its worship to the surrounding culture?" The answer to this question goes back to a basic assumption in Christianity. The principles of Christianity are above culture, for Christianity transcends all culture. When persons become Christians, their first task is to make Christ real in their lives. At the same time they must apply Christianity to their culture—to their world of family, work, education, and relaxation. This second step is to "inculturate" Christianity into their lives and culture. The process begins with individuals, but becomes a corporate process as many individuals are saved within the local church. Therefore, the worship of the individual will express his or her culture—expressing the "worthship" to God that is due Him with the individual's own words, thought patterns, and cultural limitations. While this is an "inculturation," it is not the same thing as the process of "contextualization." I am against the contemporary view that says we must change the gospel or water down the gospel, which is "contextualization."

Robert R. Redman Jr., assistant professor of theology and ministry at Fuller Theological Seminary, accuses Marva Dawn of attacking culture, by making it "a demonization of popular culture that makes culturally relevant worship difficult if not impossible."[7] Dawn would answer the charges against her by saying that worship in Western civilization, specifically worship in the European traditions, has profoundly shaped culture. She would claim that when we follow the liturgical European tradition, we are following Christianity that transcends culture. She maintains that the worship patterns of the historical Protestant church influenced the European culture into becoming Christian, and worship that comes out of European culture is transcultural and transtemporal. Therefore, when we give in to contemporary worship forms, we are surrendering to culture that is not influenced by Christianity, so our worship is not Christian. She would have us vigorously defend our liturgical worship forms, vigorously implement our liturgical worship forms, and so change the culture of America back to what it was.

Area 4: Conforming to the World Versus Transforming the World

The critics of contemporary worship indicate that by surrendering to contemporary Americans—giving them what people want in worship—we have not changed them but have pandered to them.[8] Dawn warns us against "Dumbing Down" worship for people who don't know what they want, don't know what to do, and don't know why they do it. She would have us keep our worship standards elevated—stretching American worship to higher standards of excellence. Her emphasis on God as the source of worship is to be commended. She maintains that when people expose themselves to God in the act of worship, individual character is formed within the individual, and Christian community is formed within the church.

Dawn defines *character* as "doing the right thing in the right way, with the right attitude, for the right purpose because you know it is right." The first two aspects of the definition of character indicate that you do the right thing (you worship God) in the right way (conform your methodology to God); hence, you change your life into conformity to God (you develop Christian character).

Dawn believes much of the tension over worship arises because the church has not taught proper worship habits and the proper meaning of worship to its young. By not being "submissive" to proper worship, individuals are "subverted" from godly practice and godly living. Rather than offering people worship that has the feel, volume, and appearance of culture, she wants to expose the unchurched to the church's worship culture in order to elevate them to a new understanding of life and a new appreciation of God and His church.

Area 5: Egotism Versus Community

Some critics charge that giving people the type of worship they want corrupts the authenticity of the local church. Rather than lifting people into the "community of faith" (i.e., the body of Christ), the church allows itself to be dragged down to the level of people, through marketing and advertisement to attract and win them for Christ. But in the process, we lose the mystery of the church and the "communion of the saints."

The critics see the rise of individualism illustrated when a person lifts a hand toward God separate from anyone else in the auditorium. The individual act, rather than the act in communion with others who do the same thing, does not build the church community. The same thing happens when you become one of hundreds who are praying in "prayer concert."

The critics maintain the church should sing together, pray the Lord's Prayer together, read the Scriptures together, affirm the Apostles' Creed together, and break bread together.

Area 6: Institutional Event Versus Individual Event

Some might argue that none of the six types of worship (see chapters 5 through 10) are in fact worship; rather, each is a different dynamic of worship.
- The Evangelistic model is not worship; it's evangelism
- The Bible Expositional model is not worship; it's teaching.
- The Renewal model is not worship; it's revival.
- The Body Life model is not worship; it's fellowship.
- The Liturgical model is not worship, for worship is internal.
- The Congregational model is not worship; it's an assembly of the church.

We might ask whether worship follows the Old Testament model or a New Testament model. Some claim that the worship of the commonwealth of Israel was a group event, but that New Testament worship took people individually to God. However, let us return to our definition of worship: "giving the worthship to God that is due Him." We worship both corporately and individually. We worship God both directly (by what we do, say, and respond in directed worship) and indirectly (because all we do brings glory to God). We worship God spontaneously—from the explosive emotions of the unexpected—and we worship by prepared songs, events, and prayers. We worship God knowingly and unknowingly—God is glorified when we respond according to God's principle, even when we don't cognitively realize we are giving glory to Him. We worship God in a sanctuary and in the open field.

While some may criticize the worship of another person, the key is to follow our heart as it follows the Word of God. We never alter our actions because of criticism, nor do we live by the negative opinions of others. Obviously, we listen to criticism, not because it is right but to compare it to Scriptures. We are exhorted, "Put everything to the test. Accept what is good" (1 Thess. 5:21, CEV).

Summary

The first murder grew out of an angry fight between two brothers who disagreed over worship. Was a vegetable sacrifice of God better than a blood sacrifice? While the first disagreement involved a substance question, today's disagreement is over methodology (i.e., how we worship). When you get into controversy over different ways of worship, ask yourself these questions:

1. Is this a question of *how* we worship or *who* we worship?

2. Is this a question of *preference* or *principle?*

3. Is this a question of cultural *expression* or Christian *essence?*

While "worship wars" continue, remember the words of Jesus: "He that is not against us is for us" (Luke 9:50, KJV).

PART TWO

Six Paradigms of Worship

CHAPTER FIVE

The Evangelistic Church

> The first purpose of the church is to spread the gospel and evangelize all who will accept Christ as Lord and Savior. It seems impossible to miss this clear directive of Scripture.
>
> Donald McGavran

A sense of expectation builds as the congregation gathers for the morning worship service. The success of an outreach campaign being conducted by the church is becoming evident as a larger-than-usual crowd begins filling the pews. The parking lot is filling even though many church members have parked at an area shopping mall. Ushers are having difficulty seating people in the fixed pews. A few have gone to find stacking chairs to place in the wide aisles. These kind of problems seem to bring joy to church members. Today will indeed be a special opportunity.

As the piano begins playing a lively gospel hymn, choir members make their way to the platform. They remain standing as the song leader moves to the pulpit. He asks the gathered crowd to take their hymn book and stand together as they sing the familiar hymn, "Amazing Grace." The people quickly respond by standing as the musicians play the last line of the hymn. Then, from all parts of the building, the words of Newton's hymn ring out.

> Amazing grace, how sweet the sound,
> that saved a wretch like me.
> I once was lost, but now am found;
> was blind but now I see.

In the hymn book, the word *Amen* follows the text of the last verse, but it is not sung in this church. In its place, the song leader encourages the congregation to shake hands with five people around them and tell them how much you appreciate their being there today. A happy muffled sound fills the auditorium as informal greetings are exchanged.

After the congregation sings another familiar hymn, "Old Rugged Cross," the song leader moves away from the pulpit to make room for the pastor. The pastor welcomes everyone and asks church members to raise their hands indicating those who brought a friend to church with them today. As hands are raised throughout the auditorium, several amens are heard. The pastor briefly prays for the service before the congregation is seated.

The pastor explains how the church has been preparing for this day for several weeks and expresses how much he appreciates each "friend" who took time out of his or her busy schedule to worship with them. He explains the church has a special friendship packet as a "thank-you" gift for each visitor. He asks visitors to complete a registration card. Ushers come to the front and begin passing out cards to each pew.

As visitors complete the cards, a quartet moves to the platform and begins singing a gospel song that is obviously a favorite of those gathered. The fast tempo of their music slows slightly as they sing a second song. When they are finished, the choir rises and sings a medley of two hymns.

Because it is an outreach day, the decision was made to minimize church announcements. This morning, the pastor simply encourages people to read their church bulletin and asks visitors to place their registration cards in the offering plate as it is passed. Once again, the ushers make their way to the front of the auditorium, with one usher leading the church in prayer from the pulpit before the offering is received. As the offering plate is passed, the pianist and organist play the hymn "How Great Thou Art."

As the song leader returns to the pulpit, he indicates the hymn number of the previous hymn and asks the congregation to rise as they sing the first and last verse. The song leader shares how much he appreciates the ministry of the visiting quartet and looks forward to their concert later in the day. He asks them to come once again just before the pastor shares the morning message.

The lead singer in the quartet tells how much they enjoy being at the church today and how encouraging it is to see a church so full. He explains the song they are about to sing was written by a member of their group, is featured on their new compact disc, and describes the difference Jesus makes in their lives. The slower tempo song is sung with pathos and has a moving effect on the congregation.

As the pastor begins his message, he talks about the importance of relationships. He shares briefly how friends have had a positive influence on his life and how much he appreciates his friends. "But as important as friends are," he explains, "there is one relationship which all of us need to develop." Making periodic reference to Abraham, he talks about the prospects of being a friend of God. As the message develops, other verses are read or quoted to explain the gospel and encourage those gathered to become "a friend of God."

As the sermon comes to a conclusion, the pastor asks the congregation to pray. Before praying, he says certain words church members have heard often. "With heads bowed and eyes closed, and no one disturbing the service in any way, let me ask you a question. If you were to die tonight, do you know for certain you would go to heaven? If you can answer yes, will you simply raise your hand and place it back down again." Across the auditorium, many faithful raise their hands.

"Thank you," the pastor continues. "Let me talk to those of you who could not raise your hand just then. Would you like to become a friend of God? You can do that today by simply turning from your sin and trusting Christ as your Savior. If you're not sure you have that relationship with God we've been talking about this morning, I would like to pray for you. Would you simply raise your hand and let me pray for you this morning?" Several hands are raised as the pastor pauses.

"In a moment, we are going to sing a closing hymn together," the pastor explains. "As we sing, I am going to invite those of you who would like to have a personal relationship with Christ to step out and make your way to the front of the auditorium. When you do that, someone will sit down with you and explain from the Bible how you can have the kind of relationship we've been describing today. Will you do that today? Let's stand and sing. And if you need to come today, step out now and make your way to the front."

As soon as the pastor completes his appeal, the choir begins singing "Just As I Am." Much of the congregation joins in singing the familiar invitation hymn. From various parts of the auditorium, people are making their way out to an aisle and moving forward. In the minds of many gathered, this is what church is all about!

What Is the Purpose of the Evangelistic Church?

As its name implies, the Evangelistic Church exists to accomplish the work of evangelism. Its mission is expressed in various ways: "Reaching the lost at any cost." "His last command, our first concern." Many church members use terms like *soul-winning* or *saturation evangelism* to describe the primary function of their church.

The mission of the Evangelistic Church is found in the Great Commission, "Go therefore and make disciples of all the nations, baptizing them in the name of the Father and of the Son and the Holy Spirit" (Matt. 28:19). Most evangelistic churches accomplish this task using the means implied within the commission itself. First, they "go" to the unsaved to make contact and reach them for Christ. This implies soul-winning visitation into the homes of unsaved people and/or advertisement to get them to attend their church. The unconverted are persuaded to become a Christian and believe the gospel. Then the church "baptizes" those who believe and assimilates them into the church family. Finally, they engage in the command of "teaching them to observe all things that I have commanded you" (Matt. 28:20).

The specific application of the Great Commission varies as different churches attempt to reach different people groups. In South American churches, great tent meetings are often part of the outreach strategy of an evangelistic church. Some American churches use Sunday school buses or soul-winning visitation to reach their community for Christ. Others launch significant media campaigns to saturate their community with the gospel. Still others reach out to the unchurched Harrys and Marys of their community through carefully planned seeker services designed to put the unsaved at ease so they can hear and understand the gospel.

Expectations and Roles in the Evangelistic Church

Because of the nature of the Evangelistic Church, the pastor is more an evangelist who preaches the gospel than a pastor in the traditional sense. He is the leader who motivates the church in highly effective soul-winning endeavors and the administrator who organizes great outreach campaigns. Success in ministry for pastors of evangelistic churches is often measured by the number of recorded conversions, baptisms, or net growth of the church over the preceding year. When the church ceases to be effective in reaching significant numbers of people for Christ, it is usually viewed as a sign of God withdrawing His hand of blessing from the church. When that happens, one of two things follow. First, the pastor may begin addressing perceived sin in the church family, which is viewed as hindering God in reaching people. Second, the pastor may be viewed as having lost his anointing, and therefore he is responsible for the lack of evangelism.

When worshipers come to church on Sunday morning, they expect there will be a clear presentation of the gospel. If the Evangelistic Church is seeker sensitive, people expect the church service to be comfortable to those attending who may be unsaved. If the Evangelistic Church follows the model described at the beginning of this chapter, worshipers expect an upbeat feel to the worship service concluded with people responding to the invitation.

The Bonding Agent of the Evangelistic Church

A pastor's reaction to a lack of response during an invitation is typical of those with the unique evangelism common in Evangelistic Churches. These pastors and their followers are deeply committed to the ministry of evangelism and are often very pointed in confronting situations they feel need to be addressed. This gift mix is expressed in the mission statement of one evangelistic church that described itself as "preaching the Word of God as it is to people as they are."

Evangelism is communicating the gospel in the power of the Holy Spirit to unconverted persons at their point of need so they can put their trust in Christ for salvation and become members of His church. These conversions take place as individuals repent of their sin and put their trust in God through Jesus Christ, accepting Him as their Savior. Normally, those who are converted determine to serve the Lord in the fellowship of a local church. Those who are gifted in evangelism are effective in making disciples of various types of people through their personal evangelistic efforts.

During the late sixties, I began compiling lists of the largest and fastest growing churches in America. *America's Fastest Growing Churches* described churches that rose to prominence because of their commitment to and effectiveness in reaching their communities for Christ.[1] Pastors like Rick Warren, Bill Hybels, Lee Roberson, Richard Lee, and Jerry Falwell are widely recognized as pastoral leaders of evangelistic churches.

The Strengths and Contributions of the Evangelistic Church

The strength of the Evangelistic Church is found in its commitment to evangelism. Most pastors of evangelistic churches would agree with

Spurgeon's claim, "There is no wrong way to win people to Christ." As a result, evangelistic churches have produced outreach ministries that have become prototypes for others committed to evangelism. In recent decades, several highly effective outreach ministries have been born out of the evangelistic zeal of these churches.

Before the 1950s, local church evangelistic crusades were a highly effective means of reaching people for Christ. Churches would erect tents on their property or conduct weeklong evangelistic meetings. The gospel was preached, and people were won to Christ. Also, great youth rallies would be held on Friday and/or Saturday evenings through which similar results were achieved among students.

Visitation evangelism was a widely used means for reaching people for Christ. On a designated evening, evangelistic teams would go out from the church to visit prospects for salvation. If there were no prospects, visitors would simply knock on doors "cold turkey" to look for those who might prove to be prospects for the gospel.

During the 1960s, Sunday school buses were being widely used to reach people for Christ. Long bus routes were established, and bus captains spent most of their Saturdays knocking on doors to find riders for their Sunday school buses the following day. In some churches, more than a hundred children would come to church from a single bus route. By the peak of the busing movement, many churches were purchasing Sunday school buses assuming the bus itself would result in increased attendance.

During the seventies and eighties, many other evangelistic strategies were developed and used to reach people for Christ—coffeehouses and concerts, telemarketing and television, drive-in films, and bumper stickers. Some proved to be more effective than others in achieving their desired end, but all were born out of the vision of evangelistic churches. Denominations composed largely of evangelistic churches experienced significant growth as new churches were established to reach new communities. Indeed, starting new churches appears to be the most effective means of reaching people for Christ.

Most recently, evangelism along existing social networks has been recognized as the most effective evangelistic strategy used by these churches. This involves reaching friends, relatives, associates, and neighbors for Christ. Church growth research suggests these are the people most likely to attend a church when invited to do so.

The Weaknesses of the Evangelistic Church

If evangelistic churches have been highly effective at getting new converts into the church, they have been less successful at keeping them there. Many churches baptize hundreds of converts a year but realize a net increase of only fifty or so new attenders. While every community has an element of transition in it, evangelistic churches tend to turn over members faster than the rate which may be more typical of their community.

Several factors may contribute to this obvious problem. First, many evangelistic churches lack the infrastructure to assimilate new converts into the church family. When a young man is converted, he is less likely to remain in the church if he attends church in a large auditorium than if he becomes a member of a smaller cell group. Also, some evangelistic churches have confused "decision making" with "disciple making." Ten people may make a decision for Christ during a soul-winning campaign but the fact that most of them never attend church suggests they may not have decided to become disciples. Finally, the constant emphasis on evangelism is often accompanied by a lack of emphasis on the disciplines of the Christian life. Those who sense a need to grow in their Christian life often leave the church that brought them to Christ and attend another church that will teach them what they need to continue growing in Christ.

Tapping into the Strength of the Evangelistic Church

Evangelism is the work of the whole church, and the whole church is involved in the process of bringing people to personal faith in Christ. This approach to evangelism is sometimes called "team evangelism." It is this approach to evangelism that is at the heart of evangelistic crusades or outreach campaigns. Every church can tap into the strength of the Evangelistic Church by teaching the principles of team evangelism and applying them in an outreach campaign.

Church growth research suggests if a person does not identify with people in the church during the two weeks after the first visit, he or she is likely to quit attending. Also, most people need to attend a church and hear the gospel for three or four weeks before they are prepared to make a decision for Christ or decide to join a church.

The Evangelistic Church attempts to carry out the fundamental principle of Christianity: getting unsaved people to become Christians. The Evangelistic Church takes on several appearances. Sometimes it looks like a seeker-driven or seeker-sensitive church with contemporary music and an up-to-date environment. Sometimes it resembles an evangelistic crusade, but it's held on Sunday morning. Whatever its appearance, it is a church committed to soul-winning and reaching every available person, at every available time, with every available means.

CHAPTER SIX

The Bible Expositional Church

A Prayer Hymn in Preparation of Worship
Break thou the Bread of life, Dear Lord to me,
As thou didst break the loaves, beside the sea;
Beyond the sacred page, I seek thee Lord,
My spirit pants for thee, O Living Word.

Mary A. Lathburg, 1841–1913

The bell rings to mark the end of Sunday school. Group members in various adult Bible study groups gather their Bibles, notebooks, and pens together and make their way to the church auditorium. Once again the teacher failed to cover all the material in the Sunday school quarterly, but no one was overly concerned. They would simply pick up where the discussion ended today when they meet again next week. Most of the Bible classes in this Sunday school planned to stretch three quarterlies of biblical content over the four quarters in the year.

As the people arrive at the auditorium, ushers are busy handing out church bulletins. Inserted in the bulletins are copies of today's sermon notes. Most church members turn to the passage being studied today and use the sermon notes to mark the text. Notes from previous weeks fall from the well-marked study Bibles as they are opened. These notes are retrieved and placed inside the back cover of the Bible. Others, better organized, leaf through their notebooks until they come to the place where the new notes should be added.

Much of the early part of the worship service is somewhat matter of fact. The hymns are sung in the order in which they are listed in the bulletin. Because of the wide variety of translations used by members of the Bible Expositional congregation, people are encouraged to follow along in their own Bibles as the Scriptures are read from the New American Standard Bible. Then a few announcements are highlighted before the offering is received. Following another hymn and a song sung by the ladies' trio, the pastor makes his way to the pulpit.

A few introductory comments soon introduce the theme of the passage being studied. Members of the congregation are encouraged to turn to the passage read earlier in the service. The sound of pages turning softly fills the hall as almost everyone has an open Bible. As the pastor begins explaining the passage, he turns on the overhead projector built into the side of the pulpit. The outline on the transparency is projected onto the screen raised high at the front of the church. Across the auditorium, many begin writing as various biblical words are defined and explained in the context of the passage.

For forty-five minutes the pastor continues explaining how the biblical writer develops his theme and why various alternate interpretations of the passage fail to take into account all the details. As the pastor moves point by point through his message, it all seems so simple. He gives various insights on the culture of that day, archaeological finds in Israel, and the shades of meaning implied in various Hebrew and Greek words. The message of the passage becomes clearer by the minute. How could any serious student of the Word miss a biblical interpretation so obvious?

By the end of the sermon, most of the congregation feel like they have a better understanding of the Scriptures in general and the passage studied in particular. Looking over the notes made in their notebooks and words highlighted in their Bible, they are impressed with the simplicity of the Word. Yet deep down inside, their appreciation for their pastor grows. They understand the Word has once again been "rightly divided" because of the gifted teaching ministry of their pastor. Although the service has ended, the study has only begun. Many will use this morning's sermon notes as the basis for their personal Bible study in the coming week. Others will use the sermon notes they anticipate collecting as they return to study the Scriptures together in the evening service.

What Is the Purpose of the Bible Expositional Church?

There is no question as to the mission and purpose of Bible expositional churches in the minds of those leading these ministries. They exist to equip believers for the work of the ministry. This is accomplished primarily through the systematic expositional preaching and teaching of the Scriptures. Describing the focus of his ministry, one pastor of a Bible expositional church writes,

> But every meeting held in the church building has been aimed at the instruction, training or worship of Christians together. Our entire Sunday School is set up to equip the saints, of all ages, to do the work of the ministry. The work of expounding and applying the Scriptures begins with the pulpit and is continued in every class, in every gathering and in many of the homes of Christians. Stress is laid upon confronting life as it is really lived with the insights and viewpoints of Scripture and drawing upon the resurrection power of an ever-present Lord.[1]

Pastor-teachers of Bible expositional churches cite various biblical precedents for their chosen ministry emphasis. Paul claimed for his own ministry, "I have not shunned to declare to you the whole counsel of God" (Acts 20:27). In his final epistle, Paul urged Timothy to "Preach the word" (2 Tim. 4:2). In the Old Testament, Ezra and the teaching priests "read distinctly from the book, in the Law of God; and they gave the sense, and helped them to understand the reading" (Neh. 8:8), and are sometimes cited as justification for this ministry model. But most involved in this approach to worship cite Ephesians 4 as the basis for their job description; pastor/teachers are viewed as gifts from God to the church "for the equipping of the saints for the work of ministry" (Eph. 4:12).

Bible expositional churches are characterized by people who know and live by the Word of God (John 8:31). They recognize and emphasize the importance of the Bible in the Christian life, beginning with salvation. Salvation involves the intellect, emotions, and will. For a person to be saved, he must know the gospel content, feel the conviction of sin and love of God, then respond by an act of the will. Because he must know the content of the gospel, expositional churches develop a strategy for teaching the Bible.

Expositional churches realize the power of an educated disciple. The effectiveness of a worker is in direct proportion to his or her education. Some workers are not successful because they have not been trained. Others fail because they have enough education but they do not know the right things (their theology is wrong). Therefore, the leader must reinforce the primacy of the Scriptures. This is the cornerstone of Christian education. He must also reinforce the primacy of the church's methods and continued loyalty to the cause of Christ. All this is accomplished through a systematic Bible-teaching ministry.

Expectations and Roles in the Bible Expositional Church

The pastor-teacher is primarily viewed as a teacher of the Scriptures. The preaching ministry of men who hold this office has been described as long and strong. They tend to practice expository preaching as the norm in their pulpit ministries. Usually this takes the form of preaching forty-five minutes to one hour each week consecutively through a book of the Bible or extended passage of Scripture.

Expository preaching would generally be defined by these men as "the proclamation of a biblical concept derived from an historical-grammatical study of a passage in its context which the Holy Spirit has first made vital in the personality of the preacher and through him applies accurately in the experience of the congregation."[2] These pastors will commonly invest fifteen to twenty hours in the preparation of a single sermon. Often the Sunday sermon comes complete with printed sermon notes and overhead transparencies used during the message.

People who attend Bible expositional churches have been conditioned to expect biblical content in the sermons they hear. Many take notes on a regular basis and carry well-marked study Bibles to church. When they leave a Sunday worship service, they expect to know more than when they came in. They look to their pastor to explain the Scriptures in an understandable manner. Unconsciously, they look for the marks of diligent study and biblical scholarship as the pastor explains the next passage in the book they are studying together.

The Bonding Agent of the Bible Expositional Church

The Bible Expositional Church is often a gift colony where those gifted in teaching gather each week. Teaching is the preparation and communication of biblical principles in the power of the Holy Spirit to others and the relevant demonstration of those principles to the specific needs represented. Those gifted in the area of teaching tend to be diligent students of the Scripture who have accumulated a thorough understanding of biblical principles as a result of their consistent study habits. In a Bible expositional church, those with the spiritual gift of teaching gather to learn from those who have developed their gift to a greater degree.

Because of their love for the study and teaching of the Scriptures, many leaders in the Bible Expositional Church are widely published authors. W. A. Criswell preached his way through the Scriptures in his first thirteen years in the pulpit of First Baptist Church, Dallas, covering Genesis 1:1 to Revelation 22:21. His sermons were collected and published as expository commentaries on the Scriptures. He was not alone in this practice. The sermons of H. A. Ironside and D. Martyn Lloyd-Jones were also published by Christian publishers and widely distributed in the Christian community. Today, a new breed of leader in this movement has writers who adapt their sermons for use in study guides to accompany daily radio broadcasts or special cassette study courses. John McArthur, Charles Swindoll, Charles Stanley, and David Jeremiah are among the best known expositional preachers expanding the influence of their ministry in this way.

The Strengths and Contributions of the Bible Expositional Church

Without question, the major strength of the Bible Expositional Church is its strong commitment to systematic Bible teaching. It would be difficult to attend one of these churches for long without increasing one's understanding of basic biblical content. Typically, these pastors follow a plan of explaining each passage in detail within the context suggested in the biblical book being studied. In following this plan, each week's message builds on the lessons learned in previous weeks. If the meaning of a passage is missed one week by the listener, it will be reviewed several times in the weeks following as other passages are explained.

Usually, the pastor's commitment to teaching the Bible extends throughout the total church ministry. The Sunday school curriculum in many Bible expositional churches tends to focus on lessons that lead the class through a book of the Bible, often as part of a multiyear plan through the entire Scriptures. While exceptions in the curriculum plan might be made at Christmas and Easter, that is not always the case. The systematic teaching of the Scriptures is viewed as more important than various seasonal themes that occur in the course of a year. Gary Inrig reflects this view when he writes,

> The complete and consecutive teaching of Scripture must receive a very high priority in assembly life. Nothing is more beneficial than a ministry of expository preaching which covers the sweep of all the books of the Bible. Bible teachers can all too easily develop pet doctrines or ride hobby horses

or carefully avoid very important, but touchy, matters. Expository preaching will keep solid food before believers and bring a balanced and nutritious diet. It is my conviction that nothing is more worthy of my best time and effort than the study and teaching of God's Word. Only God's Word quickened by His Spirit can establish believers and make them strong in Christ, and so all our church services focus upon the teaching of Scripture.[3]

The Weaknesses of the Bible Expositional Church

As is common with other worship styles considered in this book, the great weakness of the Bible Expositional Church is also closely related to its strength. These churches are so committed to the systematic teaching of the Scriptures that they tend to minimize Christian experience and evangelistic outreach. Experience is sometimes viewed as a threat to biblical authority. When mentioned in their sermons, it is most often coupled with warnings against depending upon one's experience but interpreting experiences by the Scriptures. Most pastors of these churches would reject any notion that an experience could result in new insights into the meaning of a biblical text.

While some expository preachers tend to emphasize application more than others, many view their role as primarily that of communicating content. The application of data to life is viewed as the work of the Holy Spirit and responsibility of the believer. Likewise, people are converted as the Holy Spirit draws them to Christ. If Christians are involved in the process of evangelism, it is assumed it is a ministry accomplished in the community rather than in the church. Even though many of these churches would claim to be committed to evangelism, research suggests those converted through the ministries of these churches are usually converted by church members through personal witness rather than through evangelistic sermons preached by the pastor. While these pastors are committed to the gospel and believe people should be saved, they are unlikely to emphasize an evangelistic appeal unless the gospel was the clear theme of the passage being studied.

Bible expositional churches tend to be most effective among upper-middle class communities and churches. It is widely believed that "blue-collar" churches are more open to emotional persuasion and stimuli because they serve a lower and lower-middle class clientele; whereas an upper-middle and upper class clientele responds to intellectual stimuli. If this has any validity, then the narrow appeal of the Bible Expositional Church is another of its weaknesses.

Tapping into the Strength of the Bible Expositional Church

The strength of the Bible Expositional Church is its commitment to the study and teaching of the Word of God. If God wants His people to engage in Bible study, He wants His leaders to organize and motivate His people for Bible study. Any church can tap into the strength of the Bible Expositional Church by having a plan that organizes the Bible teaching and Bible study ministries of the church. Also, the pastor and others should provide motivation to encourage people to study the Bible.

Every church should have a variety of Bible study opportunities for adults in order to give different people different opportunities. Some may prefer to study the Bible in a traditional age-graded class, whereas others would rather belong to a group with something in common other than age. Still others prefer belonging to a large auditorium Bible class or may wish to study more formally in a church-related Bible institute class.

Adult education has become a way of life in recent years, and the church needs to take advantage of this opportunity in providing courses, seminars, lectures, and other Bible study opportunities for those who wish to study the Scriptures. Many churches have found that Bible studies on such themes as marriage, training children, or financial management attract those who might otherwise not be interested in Bible study.

In organizing a variety of Bible study opportunities, some attempt should be made to coordinate various efforts and gain maximum results. In a larger church, there may be a pastor responsible for this just as a children's pastor or youth pastor might organize the educational ministries of young people. In a smaller church, this can be accomplished through the board of Christian education and the use of a master calendar in the church office. This will help avoid conflicts in programming and reduce unnecessary duplication of efforts.

People must not only have opportunity to study the Bible, they also must be motivated to take advantage of those opportunities. The best way to motivate people is to convince them a certain course of action will meet a perceived need or challenge them with a dream. Pastors have been successful in using both of these methods to engage people in meaningful Bible study.

Pastors of growing churches preach from the same Bible as pastors of churches not experiencing growth, but they are often more successful in convincing their listeners of the relevance of their message to the listener's life. If given the choice, the average churchgoer would probably rather hear a message on the topic "How to Live the Successful Christian Life" than a message on the topic "The Meaning of Baptism in Romans 6," even though both messages may be based on the same passage and have largely the same outline. People are motivated to study the Bible when they are convinced it will help them meet a need.

Bible study should also be promoted as a challenge. A young couple preparing for marriage can be challenged to study what the Bible says about relationships, finances, the home, and other marriage-related topics on the basis they want their marriage to be the best it can be. Similarly, new parents may be challenged to complete studies related to parenthood as they dream of being the best parents they can be. One pastor used to challenge his people at the annual watch night service to become an authority on some book, character, or chapter of the Bible that year. One year, a member of his congregation chose the Twenty-third Psalm. In the course of the year, that man found and studied forty-two books written on that psalm. He became so excited about his study, he went to Israel on his vacation to see how shepherds keep their sheep.

In recent years, there has been a growing interest and adoption of the practice of expository Bible preaching. Today, many leading pastors with large congregations use this approach almost exclusively. When pastors preach according to this plan, they demonstrate their commitment to the Scriptures. People are then more likely to follow their pastor's leadership in Bible study and begin studying the Scriptures consistently in their own life.

Other pastors vary their preaching topics more widely but are systematic in their Bible teaching in that they plan their church year with special emphasis during campaigns and conferences, such as church growth campaigns, stewardship campaigns, missionary conventions, prophecy, and deeper life conferences. Other pastors rely on the curriculum plan in their Sunday school to ensure a systematic program of Bible teaching is in place in their church. As pastors or Sunday school teachers teach the Scriptures in this way, they help their people grow internally through Bible study. This often leads to external church growth as others come to have their needs met in this way.

CHAPTER SEVEN

The Renewal Church

I believe we are ripe for a new reformation concerning the believers' priestly ministry. . . . Five hundred years ago the issue was relationship: restoring personal access to God. Today, it is worship: revealing the potential in our praises before God.

Jack Hayford, *Worship His Majesty*

Even though it is ten minutes before the worship service starts, the worship center is rapidly filling and several instrumentalists have already taken their places on the platform. Four singers—two men and two women—are moving toward the four microphone stands spread across the platform. Eight quick strokes on the bass drum are a prelude to the full band—two guitars, one keyboard, a trombone, baritone sax, and flute—breaking out in song. The singers move closer to the microphones and begin a rhythmic clap. Soon the whole congregation is following their lead. The words of a contemporary praise chorus are projected on the wall as the singers begin singing. Church is going to begin early this morning.

As the sound echoes throughout the worship center, enthusiasm is evident in the voices of those singing loudly. Most are smiling broadly. Whatever cares and concerns they may have had as they entered the building have now been set aside. For the next forty-five minutes, people are there to worship God.

The worship service seems to flow naturally from one song to another. There are no hymn books in the building. Instead, the words of each song are projected on the wall as each new song begins. Most are short choruses sung several times. Occasionally, one of the members of the praise team reads a verse from the Bible or leads in a brief prayer between songs. As the service continues, the music is becoming slower and softer. At one point, all the instruments cease playing as the praise team and congregation continue singing. Many sing with raised hands gently swaying to the rhythm of the song. At the invitation of the worship leader to worship the Lord, many begin praying audibly where they are.

Most of the songs sung in this service have addressed the theme of God's holiness. A female vocalist now moves to a microphone and begins singing softly one of the older hymns of the faith. "Holy, Holy, Holy, Lord God Almighty . . ." Others in the praise team accompany her about the third line of the hymn. By the end of the first verse, the worship band is playing softly. Once again words appear on the wall. The congregation joins in, hands raised, many with eyes closed, a few with tears resting on their cheeks.

As the worship time winds down, the pastor makes his way to a Plexiglas pulpit. He reminds the church he is in the midst of a teaching series on "Living in the Presence of God." He begins by reading several verses from various parts of the Bible where people express their understanding of God as a holy God. "If God is a holy God, He also calls us to be a holy people," the pastor explains. In the thirty-five minutes following, he shares seven steps to becoming a holy Christian. Each principle is stated and drawn from a verse of Scripture. Several members of the congregation list each point diligently with the appropriate verse as the message progresses.

As the pastor concludes his message, there is a special appeal to church members to apply the principles of holiness to their lives this week. Those with special needs are invited to come to the altar for special ministry. Once again the praise team and worship band is leading in the singing of familiar choruses. Many are making their way to the front of the building to pray together in small groups. Others appear to be making personal commitments in the pew as they sing. Throughout the worship center this morning, there is a sense that God is present among His people. People feel as if they have been to church today.

What Is the Purpose of the Renewal Church?

When asked why their church exists, the pastors and people of most renewal churches would simply respond, "to worship God." While the style of worship in many of their churches may be new and different, the concept is not. The old Presbyterian catechism began by identifying "the chief end of man" as that of worshiping God and enjoying Him forever. The leaders of the Renewal Church movement would argue they are simply accomplishing that objective in a manner more consistent with the culture of their times. This different approach to worship is most evident in the music used in their worship services.

When most people think of worship, their thoughts quickly turn to music. Congregational singing and church choirs and orchestras are an integral part of the worship experience of many Christians. According to hymn writer Jack Hayford,

> Worship may be possible without song, but nothing contributes more to its beauty, majesty, dignity or nobility, nor to its tenderness and intimacy. There is a full spectrum of purposes and practices of song in worship. The breadth of style, the endless melodic possibilities, the delicate nuances of choral dynamics, the brilliant luster of instrumental arrangement, the soul-stirring anthems of anointed choirs, the rumbling magnificence of giant organs—all seem clearly to be a God-given means for our endless expansion in worship. New musical expression is fitting as we each discover new things about the manifold wisdom of the Lord our God.[1]

The ultimate purpose of all church music should be to glorify God. The primary emphasis of the Book of Psalms, the hymn book of the Old Testament, was to glorify God. Because Christian experience affects the whole person, Christian music should communicate biblical content to the mind, should provoke an emotional experience, and should lead to a commitment of the will. The nature of our Christian commitment and daily walk with God should be expressed in church music.

But worship also involves a human response to the majesty of God. Music aids in worship because it helps us express our inner feelings toward God. The power of music is emphasized throughout Scripture. A song can refresh a discouraged or depressed person, bring about a state of physical well-being, and have a positive spiritual influence on a person (1 Sam. 16:23). Throughout the Scriptures, the power of music is demonstrated in that miracles are often associated with celebration in song. There were songs as Israel went out to fight major battles and songs at times of spiritual breakthroughs, such as the crossing of the Red Sea and the bringing of the gospel to Europe.

The Scriptures show music and singing as prominent in the life of the early church. The importance of singing is emphasized because it is closely linked with prayer (1 Cor. 14:15). Worship in song is also described as the normal expression of a life saturated with the Word of God (Col. 3:16) and the fullness of the Holy Spirit (Eph. 5:18).

Expectations and Roles in the Renewal Church

The role of the pastor in the Renewal Church is significantly different from that in other church ministry paradigms. The pastor is often the primary worship leader in the Renewal Church. It is not uncommon to find pastors with as much training in music as Bible and theology. Most renewal church pastors view themselves as exhorters who encourage a congregation of worshiping priests to worship their God. They approach the worship service with an enthusiastic attitude about the privilege of entering God's presence. One renewal pastor describes himself as the choir leader, the congregation as the choir, and God as the audience.

Those who attend the Renewal Church tend to agree with their pastor's view of the church. They come to church expecting to participate in the worship of God. They expect the worship team to create a good feeling experience during the service. Most congregational members in renewal churches expect a nonjudgmental, positive attitude in the church where they are free to raise their hands, bow in prayer, or worship God through some other means. Church has not been church if they do not "feel" as though they experienced God as they worship in song during the service.

There is more to the Renewal Church service than an extended time of worship in song. The worship time is unquestionably the focus of the service. This time is usually followed by an opportunity for the pastor to share from the Scriptures, but that is clearly not greater in both the minds of the pastors and congregation. If "the Spirit is moving" in the worship time, it is generally considered in bad taste to interrupt worship to make time for preaching. Some pastors of renewal churches may not preach for several weeks, but they consider this as an evidence of the moving of God in their church.

The Bonding Agent of the Renewal Church

In light of the uplifting and encouraging spirit which characterizes many renewal church services, it is not surprising that renewal churches often resemble gift colonies for those gifted in exhortation. Exhortation is the spiritual gift that glues many of these churches together. People gather week by week to encourage one another and "stir up love and good works"

(Heb. 10:24). They come together for a time of renewal in preparation for the challenges they will face between Sundays.

Exhortation is urging others to act on the basis of their faith in God, advising others how to accomplish specific goals in life and/or ministry, cautioning others against actions that are potentially dangerous, and motivating others in the Christian life and ministry. Those gifted in exhortation usually develop simple strategies to accomplish goals and effectively encourage and motivate others to remain faithful in their service for God.

In many respects, the Renewal Church is the church that meets the special needs of the baby boomer. This generation has had a strong tendency toward experience and relationship. The Renewal Church invites boomers and others to experience God in worship and to deepen their relationship with God and others. As boomers have begun returning to church, many renewal churches have experienced significant growth. As a result, many renewal pastors and worship leaders have become leading representatives for this movement and are becoming better known in Christian circles. Some of the current leaders within the Renewal Church movement include Jack Hayford, John Wimber, Graham Kendrick, and John Arnett. Although these leaders differ slightly in theology and approach to ministry, they are all involved in renewal-type ministries that emphasize experiencing God through corporate worship. Others in this movement are known more for the songs they have written than the sermons they preach. These include a growing number of singer/songwriters associated with various recording labels such as Hosanna/Integrity Music and Maranatha! Music.

The Strengths and Contributions of the Renewal Church

The strength of the Renewal Church is its emphasis on worship in song and the use of new music for a new generation of worshipers. Much of what has been written on worship in the past has been written from a liturgical perspective. Real worship was generally considered "high church," and what evangelicals did was generally considered a poor substitute. The Renewal Church movement has highlighted an alternative to liturgical worship that is apparently effective in bringing people into a deep reverence for God. In doing so, this movement has encouraged other nonliturgical worship-style churches to renew their focus on worshiping God in their Sunday worship services.

Christianity is concerned not only with the end (worship experience and transformed life) but also with the means to an end (method of worship). There are scriptural patterns for both the manner and instruments of worship. Some organizations claim they worship God, but apart from the New Testament means of worship. Among the most common method by which believers worship God corporately is the Sunday morning worship service.

One leader in the Renewal Church movement states, "A worship service is convened (1) to serve God with our praise and (2) to serve people's need with His sufficiency."[2] In the worship service, we first serve God through our worship and praise of Him. This involves assembling together (Heb. 10:25); singing unto the Lord (Ps. 96:1); and continuing in prayer, sharing, and the apostles' doctrine (Acts 2:42). This was the essence of the worship service of the early church.

Worship not only serves God, it also meets the needs of those who worship. This is due to the nature of worship in that it invites the very presence of God in the midst of the worshiping body. "You are holy, enthroned in the praises of Israel" (Ps. 22:3). Although most human needs can be met in a variety of ways, they can be best met in God, that is, through His presence and ministry in our lives.

Renewal churches are sometimes criticized because they do not sing older songs in their worship services. Although some renewal churches incorporate older hymns into their worship services, most of the music sung in these churches has been written since the 1960s. Actually, this criticism reveals the strength of the Renewal Church as a revival movement. One of the historic marks of the church in revival is the emergence of new music. The thousands of new songs written and widely used in the renewal movement may be one mark of the reality of the revival experience they are claiming.

The Weaknesses of the Renewal Church

Even with its emphasis on revival and experiencing God, the Renewal Church is not without its weaknesses. Perhaps the most often mentioned weakness of this movement is the shallowness of their experience. This shallow experience is seen in the constant shifting from trend to trend within the Renewal Church due to a lack of commitment to doctrinal focus and teaching. Over the last twenty-five years, a number of movements within the renewal movement have quickly risen, gained popularity, then passed off the scene as another movement rose to prominence.

Perhaps the most dramatic illustration of this problem in recent years is seen in the recent break between two recognized leaders in this movement, John Wimber and John Arnett. When Arnett and his Toronto Airport Vineyard became involved with what has become known as "the Toronto Blessing," their continued involvement with the unique signs and wonders of that movement, including laughing in the Spirit and animal sounds, led Wimber and the broader Vineyard movement to ask Arnett and his church to disassociate from the Vineyard. Wimber argued the Toronto church had moved outside of the worship model of the Vineyard movement. Ironically, critics of the Vineyard action argue it was a similar controversy between Wimber and Chuck Smith that resulted in the original Vineyard Christian Fellowship being asked to leave the Calvary Chapel movement.

Some leaders within the Renewal Church movement recognize this problem but argue it will resolve itself in time. The movement is young, as are many who pastor these churches. Also, many members of renewal churches are first-generation Christians who have not had the benefits of being trained in Christian homes and Sunday schools. Preaching in renewal churches focuses on building specific life skills, but there is little doctrinal teaching within these churches. As the movement continues, some leaders foresee a time when expository Bible teaching will be more common in renewal churches, leading to a greater level of maturity and doctrinal stability. Certainly the example of some renewal church leaders like Chuck Smith suggests an expositional Bible teaching ministry is not incompatible with this worship style.

Tapping into the Strength of the Renewal Church

While all six worship styles identified in this book help Christians worship God in their own way, many churches can learn how to enrich their worship experience through the Renewal Church approach to worship in song. Many of the innovations of the Renewal Church can be adapted to other worship styles. The result can be a much richer worship experience for church members as they gather for the Sunday morning worship service.

A word of warning: Many church leaders have made the mistake of trying to change the worship style of their church too quickly or for the wrong reasons. This action has resulted in increased tensions in the church and actually hindered the corporate worship experience of the church. The way one worships God is very close to that person's perception of himself or herself. Often, attempts to change one's worship style are viewed as a challenge to the worshiper, suggesting his or her worship is inferior and/or unacceptable to God. This does not mean worship styles cannot be changed or modified; only that care should be taken to ensure these changes are implemented correctly.

The worship leader and praise team are keys to introducing new music into a worship service. The music leader is responsible for teaching worship to the congregation. The praise team is usually an ensemble of three to nine singers who lead the congregation in worship. In some churches, the church choir serves as a praise team to lead the congregation in worship.

New music should be introduced in a worship service for the right reasons. New music should not be sung simply because it is new. Nor should older songs be omitted simply because they are old. Rather, the selection of music for the worship service should be based on the theme and focus of worship in that service. The songs selected should help the congregation worship some aspect of the greatness of God, regardless of when they were written.

Although the worship services of many renewal churches appear informal, the appearance of informality is really the result of many hours of careful planning and preparation. This planning results in continuity in the service and helps the worship team make appropriate transitions from one phase of worship to the next. In a well-planned worship service, the congregation is led comfortably from one song to the next with minimal interruptions. This continuity helps people remain focused in their worship of God.

In planning a worship service, several factors should be considered. First, songs are selected along a common theme. When possible, the worship service is most effective when the sermon theme is evident in the words of each song used. Second, care should be taken to arrange songs by keys. Worship leaders usually try to change keys as few times as possible during the worship time. When changes have to be made, modulating up by half steps usually works best. Care should be taken to avoid singing songs written in keys outside the singing range of the congregation.

Tempo is another consideration in arranging songs for worship. Usually, it is best to move from a faster tempo to a slower tempo in the worship service. In doing so, worship leaders should take care to change the meter of the songs used as few times as possible. One area in which change can be helpful is in the texture or accompaniment used with each song. Various musical instruments including piano, organ, and guitar could be used with different songs. Also, some songs may be sung a cappella. Some worship leaders will have only men or women sing a verse of a hymn or chorus.

In planning worship services, care should be taken to create a unique "feel" to the service. The worship mood should be compatible with the predominant worship style of the congregation. Some churches like to worship with fast-moving songs and sing loudly. Other churches are more reflective in their worship mood. The most effective worship service in many churches is one which falls somewhere between. A wise worship leader will take care to plan worship services that enable the congregation to worship God in spirit and truth.

Many renewal churches require their worship teams to practice as a preparation for ministry. During this practice, the worship leader can lead the praise team through the service and make minor changes as necessary to ensure a smooth flow. The leader should avoid excessive talking between songs or leaving blank spots between songs. When possible, instrumentalists should play musical bridges between songs that do not flow together naturally.

Even the most conservative congregation can be encouraged to sing newer music and expand their worship experience. When teaching new music, it is best to do it over several weeks. The congregation can be exposed to the music as the instrumentalists play it before or after a worship service, or perhaps during the offering. The next week, the choir might sing the new song as special music in a church service. Later, the song could be introduced in congregational singing at an appropriate place in the worship service.

A teenager once complained to his father that all the hymns sung in church were old and stuffy. The father responded, "If you think you can do better, do it." Responding to his father's challenge, Isaac Watts retired to his room and wrote his first hymn. In the years since, God has used many others to write hymns to help us express praise and worship to Him. As we plan our worship services, we should use the best songs available from every generation and culture to help us worship God.

CHAPTER EIGHT

The Body Life Church

In all things grow up to be like Christ, who is our head. His body is made up of many believers and is held together as each individual supports one another, helps one another, and builds up one another, so that each individual grows in character to maturity and the whole body grows to completion as all individuals complete their appointed tasks and roles.

Ephesians 4:15–16, Author's Translation

It is almost seven-thirty Thursday evening, and six families have already arrived at a gray brick home at the corner of Elm Street and Maple Avenue. Nine children have gathered around the television in the basement recreation room to watch a video. Upstairs, their parents have begun talking informally in the living room. As another couple arrives, one group member asks the others to share the "highs" and "lows" of the previous week. One by one, group members share recent events and news that brought them great joy or sorrow.

As the sharing concludes about fifteen minutes later, another group member reaches for his guitar as his wife suggests they sing a familiar chorus. During the next ten minutes, the group sings praise choruses, which are well known among most group members. The other members quickly catch on to the repetitive words and simple melody. A few group members raise their hands as they worship in song. Others close their eyes and sing meditatively.

"Just before we begin tonight's Bible study," the group leader announces, "there are a few things I need to share with you." He reminds group members that the children's ministry could use a few workers during Sunday morning worship. Also, next month their cell group is responsible for the nursing home ministry. The group agrees to bring lunch and eat together at the church on the appointed Sunday before going to the nursing home to visit. Three people offer to get together and provide music for the meeting. The group leader asks another group member if he will share a ten-minute message with the seniors. Parents are encouraged to bring their children with them because the seniors seem to enjoy visits from the children most.

"Let me share something I read earlier this week," says the group leader. After reading a short paragraph from a devotional book, the leader continues. "As I read this, I thought about the chapter we are studying this week in our study guide." By now most of the group have opened well-worn paperback study guides written by a popular Bible teacher. Looking around the room, several books appear to have passages marked and highlighted.

For the next half hour or so, the conversation seems to flow well with each group member taking part. Several share insights that struck them in their personal study during the past week. Others share experiences that seem to confirm the veracity of those insights. Occasionally, someone raises a question. "That sure sounds good, but how are we going to do that when both my husband and I have to work forty hours a week to keep up with the mortgage?" Several group members nod in agreement as two group members suggest strategies that appear to be working for them.

Throughout the discussion, the group leader has not said much. On one occasion when the group begins to wander off course, he introduces a new question to get them back to the study guide. Now he looks at his watch and interrupts again. "This is a great discussion tonight, but the time is getting late. I think it would be good to take some time to pray together before we bring things to a close. Does anyone have any specific prayer requests they would like to mention?" he asks.

In the next few minutes, several group members mention various situations they would like to have the group pray about. The group leader notes one family is absent tonight because the father was laid off and suggests the group pray for them. He waits for a group member to begin the prayer. For the next twenty minutes, several group members pray aloud for the various needs that had been raised earlier. Many also take time to thank God for the cell group and how much being a part of the group means to them. About half the prayers offered mention the pastor, other church leaders, and the Sunday services.

As the group leader concludes his prayer, group members make their way toward the kitchen. Each week a different person is responsible for refreshments. This week, the snack consists of three varieties of cookies, coffee, tea, and soft drinks. This group will meet Sunday with several hundred other church members in the local high school auditorium. For most gathered in this home, though, these Thursday night meetings are the primary worship experiences of their week. The pastors of the Body Life Church they attend each week not only think that's acceptable, they are constantly stressing the need for everyone in the church to be part of a small group.

What Is the Purpose of the Body Life Church?

Various churches define their mission in different ways. Most advocates of the Body Life Church would define their purpose and mission in the context of fellowship. The focus of the cell group and corporate gatherings of believers is to enhance the quality of fellowship among believers.

Ray Stedman, author of *Body Life,* describes this approach to ministry, noting, "Perhaps the best term for it is commonality, the clustering of Christians together in a shared intimacy that, rather mysteriously, forms a clear channel for the moving of the Spirit of God in power. . . . It is this shared intimacy with one another and the Lord which is the missing note in today's church life."[1] Likewise, another leader in this movement writes, "Very little is said in the New Testament about evangelism in the church; that is, where believers gather to be edified. This is of course a New Testament norm. Generally speaking, unsaved people are to be reached by the church, not in the church."[2]

When the New Testament talks about fellowship, often the reference is to the believer's fellowship with God. This fellowship is foundational to a second dimension of fellowship identified in the New Testament church—that which exists between believers. This aspect of fellowship is identified by two Greek words translated "fellowship," the emphasis on the unity of the church, and the evidence of fellowship cells in the early church.

Two principle Greek words are used in the New Testament to describe fellowship. The first is *koinonia,* which is translated "communion" and "fellowship" in the New Testament and has the idea of "sharing in common." The second word translated "fellowship" is *metoche.* This word literally means "partnership" and conveys the idea of sharing in or partaking in something as one of the partners of an enterprise.

The idea of Christian fellowship is also conveyed in the affirmations of unity in the early church. The Greek word *henotes,* meaning "unity" or "oneness," is used only twice in Scripture (Eph. 4:3, 13), but the concept is emphasized in the Book of Acts by the expression "one accord" (Acts 1:14; 2:1; 4:24) and statements concerning the church being "of one heart and one soul" (Acts 4:32).

As one studies the pattern of church growth in the early church, there appear to be two aspects of church life:

1. The cell, which was the smaller group meeting together as a fellowship group or ministry team (Acts 4:32);

2. The celebrative gathering of the cells in a larger group for some corporate activity (Acts 5:14).

Evidence for the existence of cells and celebration as part of church life exists in the New Testament apart from the church in Jerusalem. The church of Corinth was apparently composed of a number of Gentile cells (Rom. 16:4) and a number of Jewish cells (Rom. 16:16). It is significant that in writing to the Romans from Corinth, the apostle sends greetings from "the whole church" in Corinth (Rom. 16:23).

Cells provide the infrastructure needed to build a larger church. Most people will be bonded to a cell group in the church before they become a part of a larger ministry. But there must also be a place for celebration. The two are complementary, not contradictory. What is learned in cells is expressed in celebration. What is gained in celebration should strengthen the cell experience.

The cell group in a Body Life Church is usually characterized by four principles.

1. Cell group members have a basic commitment to one another and their cell group.

2. Cell group members are committed to openness in relationships, especially within the context of the cell group. Often, this takes time to develop, and grows the longer people are involved in a cell group.

3. The cell group serves as the accountability structure in the lives of its members. People in these groups build a reliance on each other.

4. Cell groups must be committed to enlargement and growth. Cells are usually divided when attendance consistently reaches eighteen to

twenty members. If a cell group does not reach this point within eighteen months, many churches elect to dissolve the group and incorporate group members into healthy growing cells.

Expectations and Roles in the Body Life Church

The pastor of a Body Life Church is the facilitator of the church. Most Body Life Churches believe in and practice the plurality of elders. There may be many "teaching elders" within a single church. On some occasions, a strong teaching pastor may emerge as the leading pastor. On other occasions, the teaching pastors in a church work to avoid allowing any one pastor to emerge as a leader. Also, most Body Life Churches have a network of lay pastors responsible for leadership in the cell group ministry of the church. These lay pastors also fulfill the role of facilitator in cell group discussions. They view themselves as part of the body primarily responsible for encouraging others to share in ministry of the body.

People who attend Body Life Churches come expecting to interact with others. During the worship service, they expect to be taught biblical principles that will help them live the Christian life. This expectation carries over into the cell group meeting. Bible study focuses on life application. The cell holds members accountable to grow in their Christian life and provides the support system lacking in many urban centers.

In the past, families have been the foundational unit in the social fabric of America. In small towns, many extended families live in the same community, sometimes on the same street. With the increased mobility of the present generation, the extended family network is breaking down. Parents struggling with the challenges of raising their children do not always have parents, grandparents, and other relatives living nearby. In Body Life Churches, the cell group becomes a kind of adopted family to which group members can turn for support and help to face the challenges of life and living.

The Bonding Agent of the Body Life Church

The small group, or cell, is the key to the infrastructure of a Body Life Church. These cells involve people in the lives of others and provide a context in which the "one another" ministries of the New Testament can be accomplished. Those attracted to this worship style tend to be gifted in the area of showing mercy.

Showing mercy is discovering emotionally stressed and distressed individuals and ministering to their emotional needs. Mercy-showers express sympathy, empathy, and spiritual ministry to help alleviate the inner pain that is causing a person's dysfunctional emotional response. Those gifted in showing mercy tend to be drawn toward hurting people and are somewhat effective in helping others rebuild their lives.

Various leaders of Body Life Churches have become well known because of the success of their churches and the popularity of their books. Larry Richards, Ray Stedman, Gene Getz, and Joe Aldrich have all emerged as leaders in the cell church movement in America. Because cells have played a major role in the remarkable growth of the church in Korea, various Korean pastors have also become recognized leaders in this movement. The best known of these pastors is David Yonggi Cho, pastor of Yoido Full Gospel Church in Seoul, South Korea, the world's largest church.

The Strengths and Contributions of the Body Life Church

The most significant strength of the Body Life Church is its emphasis on small group ministries. These cells serve as a glue that bonds newcomers to the church. Often people have a stronger identity to their cell than to the church. The cell is often the means by which newcomers are introduced to the larger congregation.

A holistic approach to evangelism requires that provision be made for the new Christian's normal growth and development; that is, the new Christian becomes settled in or bonded to a local church. He or she then will be brought under the ministry of the Word of God that will result in spiritual growth (1 Pet. 2:2), victory over sin (Ps. 119:9–11), answered prayer (John 15:7), growth in character (1 Cor. 3:23), and strengthened faith (Rom. 10:17). The local church is also where Christians will be able to grow through fellowship with other Christians (Heb. 10:25). When a church fails in the bonding process, new Christians stop attending church regularly and the growth and development process in their life is hindered.

Bonding is essential to the task of "closing the back door of the church." Nothing is more frustrating than spending time and effort to win people to Christ and then watching them become casual church members, or join another local church, or drop out of church completely. But that is exactly what happens when the task of bonding is not taken seriously.

Bonding is a biblical pattern. The church in Jerusalem grew more rapidly than any church since that time, yet those Christians were able to keep their members in spite of the incredible persecution they faced. New Christians were bonded to the church as their felt needs were met (Acts 2:44) and they were made to feel part of the church family (Acts 2:42). Those who were already members were willing and eager to make room for the newcomers (Acts 2:47).

It is sometimes assumed that new Christians and new members are bonded to the church when they formally join. In practice, the key to the bonding process is not church membership but church ownership. Newcomers are bonded to the church only when they begin to think of the church as "my church," and that only happens when they begin to feel like a vital part of the church as a whole or some group or organization within the church.

The cell group is what keeps people from drifting through the church. These groups also reach out to others in the community. Research suggests that to remain in a church, a new believer must become part of a social group or make a relationship to someone in the church within two weeks. Therefore, networking or bonding new believers to a cell is imperative as part of an effective church growth strategy.

The Weaknesses of the Body Life Church

Just as the cell group is the strength of the Body Life Church, it can also be its greatest weakness. Many Body Life Churches are so committed to the cell group approach to ministry that they neglect other effective options that may be available to them. If a particular ministry option does not fit into the cell group model, it is probably not used by the Body Life Church. This includes ministries such as Sunday school, Vacation Bible School, outreach visitation, nursing home services, children's club ministries, large evangelistic youth rallies, and crusade evangelism. Advocates of the cell group approach to ministry argue they accomplish more ministry through cells than would be accomplished through these other ministry options. Outside observers are not always convinced.

One of the reasons people outside the Body Life Church remain skeptical is the tendency of many body life leaders to assume conclusions without verifying them with documentation. This movement was born during a period of anti-institutionalism, and many leaders responded to the mood of the times by refusing to keep records of institutional growth. It is often difficult to document the growth of Body Life Churches because they do not count attendance. Also, church leaders describe their people as maturing faster than Christians in other churches, but again these claims are made without research support. Indeed, it may be very difficult to find a tool to measure Christian maturity and then demonstrate that Christians in one church mature faster than in others. Also, it would be difficult to identify all the causal factors that resulted in the faster maturing rate even if such a phenomenon could be demonstrated.

Tapping into the Strength of the Body Life Church

If the strength of the Body Life Church is its cell group ministry, other churches can tap into the strength of this worship style by developing small group ministries as part of their broader ministry strategy. The primary analogy for the church in the New Testament is that of the body (1 Cor. 12:27–28). Just as the body grows by the division of cells, so the church grows through the division of cells. One key to ongoing church growth is adding ministries, adding ministers, and adding places of ministry. Small group ministries enable churches to add new ministries at minimal costs to the church, develop new lay ministers engaged in using their gifts in significant ministry, and provide new places of ministry both within the body and the broader community.

Various approaches to establishing small group ministries have been adopted by different churches. Some cell groups are arranged loosely by age: twenties, thirties, and so on. Other churches group people by marital and/or family status: single adults, parents of teens, and so on. Other cell groups are arranged according to unique needs of group members, such as single parents and military wives. In some regional churches, people are assigned to cell groups in the communities in which they live. Many churches adopt an open policy and end up with cell groups that may fit any of the above patterns.

Cell groups are most effective when they are established for a purpose. Some groups begin as an evangelistic home Bible study. As group members are converted, the group becomes a discipleship group. Later, that group may be divided into several evangelistic groups, or the purpose of the group will change again. In many larger groups, cells are organized for a fellowship purpose. People are encouraged to get to know one another better in a small group setting. Teaching is another purpose around which cell groups commonly meet.

When introducing cell groups to your church, it is important to establish a receptiveness to the idea. Some churches have quickly moved into a cell group ministry that quickly degenerated into cliques and factions. As a result, sometimes even the name "cell" is accompanied by negative connotations that must be overcome. One pastor used the acronym HOME (Homes Open for Ministry and Evangelism). A church opposed to cell groups was willing to embrace HOME groups. Dale Galloway, former pastor of New Hope Community Church, Portland, Oregon, calls his cells TLC Cells, which stand for Tender Loving Care Cells.

Christians need to be taught the value of cell groups before they are likely to become involved. Many pastors have conditioned their churches to be receptive to this approach to ministry by teaching and preaching on the "one another" ministries identified in the New Testament. The focus of such a preaching series is to demonstrate that intimate involvement in the lives of fellow believers was part of the norm of New Testament Christianity. These types of ministries can best be accomplished through cell groups.

CHAPTER NINE

The Liturgical Church

We praise Thee, O God:
We acknowledge Thee to be the Lord,
All the earth doth worship Thee, the Father everlasting.
To Thee all angels cry aloud;
The heavens and all the powers therein,
To Thee cherubim and seraphim continually do cry;
Holy, Holy, Holy Lord God of Sabaoth.
Heaven and earth are full of the majesty of Thy glory,
The glorious company of the apostles praise Thee,
The goodly fellowship of the prophets praise Thee,
The noble army of martyrs praise Thee.

Affirmation of Faith
The Te Deum of the Church

About five minutes before eleven, worshipers begin silently finding their places in the pews of the old church at the corner of Main and Washington Streets. Sunlight filters through the stained-glass windows. The organist has taken her place in the balcony and for the past fifteen minutes has been softly playing arrangements from Mozart's more familiar themes. With bowed heads, those gathered in the pews below are aware of the soothing music as they reflect on the activities of recent days and prepare their hearts to worship God. Atmospheric worship is important in the Liturgical Church.

Children do not run or talk in the sanctuary because it is the Lord's house. They are in the presence of God. People do not whisper or make any irreverent motion in the sanctuary.

Two women sit together back on the left. They had spent much of the weekend together helping four other women in the church sort out donated clothing for a special missions project in Mexico. As they packed the clothes, each of the ladies in the mission circle had expressed surprise at how much had come in from the church. Corporate donations from several businesses owned by church members would certainly cover the cost of transporting the boxes of clothes quickly to the missionaries who would distribute them to those who need them most.

Worshipers were again reminded of the generosity of the church late Saturday morning as they helped stock the shelves of the church food bank. While member donations of canned goods, cereals, and powdered milk were helpful, these women were also aware of the food vouchers from a neighborhood grocery store that were included in each box. Although the minister had not indicated how the church had obtained them, they had it on good authority that the regular gift from the grocery store was the result of the minister's personal efforts to ensure the poor in the community had groceries.

On the second row, the thirty-two-year-old man sitting with his wife and children is thinking about the Monday evening little league ball game he will be coaching. As a child he had enjoyed baseball and dreamed of some-day playing for the Yankees. He never did play the game well enough to entertain such hopes. Two summers ago he began assisting the coach of his son's ball team. Although his involvement as an elder in the church keeps him busy, he feels it is important to take time to help young boys pursue their dreams of playing in the major leagues. He knows his other responsibilities at the church will not excuse him from this summer project.

As eleven o'clock approaches, the robed choir takes their place on either side of the platform. They are followed by the minister, who is wearing his distinctive Geneva preaching robe. As the choir leader makes his way to the podium on the right, the organist plays the Call to Worship. The congregation rises and begins singing.

> Praise God from whom all blessings flow.
> Praise Him all creatures here below.
> Praise Him above ye heavenly hosts.
> Praise Father, Son, and Holy Ghost. Amen.

As the congregation concludes, the minister prays the Invocation—a prayer to invoke the presence of God in their worship service. Next, he asks the congregation, "Christian, what do you believe?"

The congregation—men, women, and children—rise to their feet and repeat in unison,

> I believe in God the Father Almighty, maker of heaven and earth: And in Jesus Christ His only Son, our Lord; who was conceived by the Holy Ghost, born of the Virgin Mary, suffered under Pontius Pilate, was crucified, dead, and buried; He descended into hell; the third day He rose again from the dead; He ascended into heaven, and sitteth on the right hand of God, the Father Almighty; from thence He shall come to judge the quick and the dead.
>
> I believe in the Holy Ghost, the holy catholic church, the communion of saints, the forgiveness of sins, the resurrection of the body, and life everlasting. Amen.

Next they cite in unison the Lord's Prayer. To some, the words hold little significance. Others speak the words softly from a heart deeply moved in the worship of God.

The minister reads the Scripture lesson from the Old Testament, followed by the New Testament reading. Then the congregation turns to the back of the hymnal for the responsive reading. The pastor and congregation alternate in reading the passages.

A classical anthem is sung by the choir, and then an organ recital is given during the offering. Next there is the singing of another of the great hymns, followed by a brief children's sermon (a story told to the children by the minister before they make their way to children's church). Using one of the parables of Jesus, the minister stands behind the podium on the left of the sanctuary and challenges the people to hear and apply the moral truths of the Scriptures to life.

At the conclusion of the sermon, the pastor directs the congregation to the hymn book. The congregation is invited to respond to the sermon in worshiping God. The hymn, written three hundred years earlier, expresses a theme remarkably similar to that which had just been preached. The choir leader directs the congregation to stand. As the final verse of the hymn comes to a conclusion, the pastor makes his way to the podium to pronounce the benediction. He raises his arms and recites the words of the Aaronic Blessing.

> The Lord bless thee, and keep thee:
> The Lord make His face to shine upon thee;
>   and be gracious unto thee:
> The Lord lift up His countenance upon thee,
>   and give thee peace. Amen.

As he concludes the blessing, the choir sings the Sevenfold Amen. The congregation quietly sits in their pews, bowing their heads in silent prayer and reflecting on the worship experience of the past hour.

What Is the Purpose of the Liturgical Church?

The Liturgical Church has a twofold ministry emphasis. The first part of its mission may be defined in the context of serving God and ministering to others. The word *liturgy* is derived from the Greek verb *latreuo* meaning "to serve." In pagan Greek cultures, this word was used most often in the context of serving the gods or serving in the name of the gods. In a Christian context, this word describes two aspects of our worship: (1) we serve God with our praises and worship; (2) as we serve others in the name of God, we express our worship of God in practical ways. Serving God with worship is the emphasis of the Liturgical Church. This is why it is called the worship service.

In the process of serving others in the name of God, the second aspect of the mission of the Liturgical Church emerges. Many liturgical churches view themselves as a prophetic voice in the community, striving for social justice on behalf of all people. The minister of a Liturgical Church is often the first pastor in a community to preach sermons addressing current social issues. Also, members of liturgical churches often take a leading role in developing and implementing strategies for reforming society and addressing social problems. Throughout history, leaders and members of liturgical churches have been involved in the abolition of slavery, the women's suffrage movement, the civil rights movement, the pro-life movement, and the religious right. As in any other church type, one's doctrinal convictions and personal political views dictate which side of a social issue a person adopts, but members of liturgical churches have historically been more likely to become actively involved in trying to change an issue than members of other church types.

Because the focus of the Liturgical Church is ministry, it is important to understand the nature of ministry. Ministry may be defined as "communication of the gospel to people at a point of need." Someone has simplified this definition claiming ministry is "finding a need and meeting it . . . finding a hurt and healing it." As important as biblical truth and doctrine is, God never intended it to be an end in itself. Rather, theology is the foundation of our ministry as we apply biblical truth to specific needs in the lives of others. Only then can a significant and lasting change be effected in the lives of others.

Expectations and Roles in the Liturgical Church

The term most often used to describe the pastor of a liturgical church is *minister*. This reflects the primary ministry function of the pastor of this church as a servant of the people. In a liturgical church, the minister is viewed as the one who is available to assist congregational members with baptisms, confirmations, weddings, funerals, pastoral counseling, hospital visitation, nursing home services, and a host of similar functions. His service to the church is not limited to adult members. In many liturgical churches, he is also involved in the church's youth ministry and prepares a weekly children's sermon as part of the morning service. The minister is indeed "all things to all people."

Those who attend liturgical churches have different expectations than those who choose to attend other types of churches. They are looking for practical ministry opportunities. Although they may sometimes complain that they are always doing something with the church, they also find a sense of personal fulfillment in their church work. Church work in many liturgical churches involves a host of traditional charitable activities, including collecting for food banks, clothing depots, missionary gift packs, and Christmas toy and food baskets. Christians in liturgical churches are often eager to express their faith in acts of practical service to others.

Christians who attend liturgical church services also expect church to "feel like church." When Elizabeth I ascended the throne of England, she faced a unique dilemma. She had been raised in a Roman Catholic faith tradition and had come to appreciate the richness of that worship style, but the position of the Catholic Church concerning her father's divorce meant she could not be queen if England remained Catholic. England had a growing Protestant movement, but Elizabeth did not feel like she had really been in church when she attended Protestant services. In her attempt to harmonize this tension and bring religious unity to England, the queen proposed what has become known as "the Elizabethan settlement" and created the Anglican Church. This new English church would retain the Catholic liturgy but adopt Protestant doctrine. England adopted the Protestant cause without abandoning the tradition of worship that had developed over fifteen hundred years.

The Bonding Agent of the Liturgical Church

One of the reasons these six worship styles have emerged today is the practice of gift colonization. Liturgical churches tend to emerge and become strong when the spiritual gift of serving is strong. Serving is discerning and meeting the spiritual and physical needs of individuals. Those gifted in this ministry are supportive of others and are concerned with helping them in any way possible. They usually enjoy manual tasks. Often they are most comfortable worshiping God in a liturgical church.

History is a second factor in the worship of the Liturgical Church. Because the development of worship traditions takes time, most liturgical churches are found among the older denominations. It is not uncommon to find church members who are the third or fourth generation of a family attending a particular church. Among ethnic groups involved in liturgical churches, families may have identified with a particular denomination for several generations. The strength of the Presbyterian church not only in Scotland but also in China and Korea is reflected in the number of immigrants from those countries that gravitate toward Presbyterian churches in North America. Similarly, many immigrants from Northern Europe gravitate toward Lutheran churches in America.

The strength of liturgical churches and the tendency of liturgical church members to become actively involved in their society has resulted in many leaders emerging in this movement. Henrietta Mears and Peter Marshall are two Presbyterian leaders who made a significant impact on American church life in the first part of this century. More recently, D. James Kennedy, Lloyd Ogilvie, and Robert Schuller are widely recognized leaders of liturgical churches. Internationally, D. Martyn Lloyd-Jones and Francis Schaeffer were widely respected leaders within their lifetimes. Anglican Bishop Desmond Tutu of South Africa was awarded the Nobel

Prize several years ago for his efforts to bring about an end to apartheid in South Africa.

The Strengths and Contributions of the Liturgical Church

One of the strengths of the Liturgical Church is the rich tradition of its worship. With the growth in popularity of contemporary praise music, many churches worship God in a manner that assumes the Holy Spirit did not move Christians to worship God before the 1960s. Other churches limit their worship to the popular hymns of the nineteenth and twentieth centuries. Liturgical churches worship God using a worship tradition of two millennia. The historic creeds, ancient hymns, and the English Psalter are commonly part of a liturgical church worship service, though they are virtually ignored in other worship styles.

Critics often allege that "high church" services are filled with empty and/or vain traditions. But is this always true? Some may recite the Lord's Prayer or the Apostles' Creed without thinking about the words, but others find this recitation helps them express themselves to God in prayer, and the reciting of a creed helps them express their faith in God. The words of Psalm 100 can be a meaningful expression of worship and praise, not only when sung to a contemporary melody but also when sung as arranged by Isaac Watts, the Scottish Psalter, a medieval chant, or a Latin hymn. Various musical arrangements will appeal to different people. This appeal has more to do with personal preference and taste in music than one's spirituality or lack of spirituality.

"God is Spirit, and those who worship Him must worship in spirit and truth" (John 4:24). Advocates of the liturgical approach to worship might argue true worship is more likely when the rich variety of worship traditions from all ages and cultures are incorporated. To limit one's worship of God to one worship style popular in a particular culture at a particular time may hinder one from worshiping God in spirit with integrity. But when many worship traditions are available to the worshiper, he or she is more likely to identify with one of those options and worship God appropriately.

A second strength of the Liturgical Church is its commitment to ministry. Most liturgical churches incorporate a wide variety of ministries designed to meet various social needs in their community as a part of their service to the community. Whereas ministry in many churches primarily serves the needs of church members, a significant portion of the typical ministry of the Liturgical Church is concerned with meeting needs of those outside the church's membership. While this does not always translate into church attendance by recipients of the church's ministry, it does improve the influence of the church in the community. For this reason, the minister of the Liturgical Church is often contacted by nonchurch families in times of transition, such as weddings, childbirth, job loss, and funerals. This provides ministers of liturgical churches a unique ministry opportunity that may prove fruitful in reaching people for Christ and increasing church attendance.

The Weaknesses of the Liturgical Church

While ministry to the community is one of the strengths of the Liturgical Church, it can also be viewed as an expression of one of its significant weaknesses. Liturgical churches often lack an evangelistic outreach. Pastor D. James Kennedy and the Coral Ridge Presbyterian Church is a liturgical church with a strong evangelistic outreach, proving that the two are not incompatible. Still, many liturgical churches emphasize social ministry to the exclusion or near exclusion of evangelistic ministries. As a result, many evangelicals view liturgical churches as lacking evangelistic zeal.

Once again, one of the strengths of this worship style contributes to its weakness. Many liturgical churches are part of older denominations with a rich history of worship traditions. Part of that history reaches back into the early years of the twentieth century when most denominations engaged in the fundamentalism/modernism controversy. In most denominations, liberalism or modernism won this struggle in the seminaries; within a generation many denominational pulpits were occupied by ministers who denied the essentials or fundamentals of the faith. Today, many liturgical churches have adopted theological positions that are incompatible with evangelistic fervor. This lack of sound biblical teaching coupled with a tendency to address the social ills of society often leaves little room for evangelism.

Tapping into the Strength of the Liturgical Church

Despite significant doctrinal differences between some liturgical churches and their evangelical counterparts, many evangelical churches would be wise to incorporate some of the strengths of this worship style into their ministries. Evangelical churches can do this in two areas: (1) we can learn to appreciate the rich worship traditions of other eras and cultures as a part of our contemporary worship of God; (2) we can learn to develop unique ministries that meet the felt needs of people in our community.

Using Historic Creeds and Hymns

There are various ways in which traditional worship expressions can be incorporated into church worship services. Some pastors have incorporated the recitation or reading of a creed, such as the Apostles' Creed, into their worship services on a short-term basis during a preaching series on that creed. A similar approach incorporates repeating the Lord's Prayer into a church service during a preaching series on that topic. Also, many pastors of nonliturgical churches have opted to incorporate a Pauline blessing or one of the other blessings of Scripture into their benediction.

Perhaps the most common season for incorporating aspects of the liturgical approach to worship into other worship styles is the Christmas season. The use of carols represents a music style more common to another era than that of contemporary worshipers. The example of Christmas demonstrates that nonliturgical church members can find rich meaning in liturgical worship styles. The wise worship planner periodically looks for hymns, carols, and choruses written in other cultures and times to add variety to the church's worship experience. When used appropriately and blended with the usual worship style of the congregation, the total worship experience can be more meaningful. A common example of this practice is seen in the use of the fifth-century Latin hymn "O Come, All Ye Faithful!" *(Adeste Fideles),* which is often sung as part of a series of choruses in many renewal congregations. Some people in those congregations might argue that the singing of Latin hymns would hinder worship without realizing that they themselves have used *Adeste Fideles* to express their own desire to worship God.

Serving Others

A second strength of the Liturgical Church which can be adopted by other worship styles is the expression of worship in service to others. Many churches have done this to some degree with special collections of food and/or gifts for the poor at Thanksgiving or Christmas. More significant ministries to address social needs in the community can also be developed by churches willing to invest the required time and effort.

Churches interested in making a significant impact on their community usually begin by investigating the unique needs of their community. Many city planning departments compile information on various neighborhoods within the city. This demographic information is usually available to business and community groups upon request. Other churches conduct community surveys to identify the felt needs of the community in which the church is located. As a result of this approach, many churches have become involved in providing a day care or after-school care ministry in their church facilities. While these ministries involve a major financial investment, other ministries may be developed with little or no cost to the church. Many churches have used their facilities for a coffeehouse/drop-in center or to conduct a midnight basketball league in an effort to help youth avoid involvement in drugs or crime. Others have developed special summer ministries, such as Vacation Bible School or camps, to assist parents in caring for children during the summer vacation. A church concerned about neglected seniors in its communities found a hot lunch program and church-sponsored bus day trips were popular among the group they had targeted to reach.

Jesus said, "For even the Son of Man did not come to be served, but to serve, and to give His life a ransom for many" (Mark 10:45). Jesus' example of ministry to others is a challenge to His disciples today. Significant ministry is an expression of our worship of God and can be used to lead others to worship God as they experience God's love through His people.

CHAPTER TEN

The Congregational Church

Thou shalt worship the Lord thy God, and him only shalt thou serve.

Matthew 4:10, KJV

Although the worship service does not begin for another twenty minutes, there are already a dozen cars crammed into the small church parking lot. It is unlikely more than one or two more cars will arrive before the service itself begins. Inside the small church building, fifty-seven people are already "in church" doing what they do every Sunday morning about this time.

They do not call it a sanctuary, but the church auditorium. Without stained-glass windows or liturgical atmosphere, it is a simple room with pews, pulpit, and a choir loft. The people are not reverently praying, but "catching up" on what has been happening in the lives of their friends. Children are having fun with their friends, yet behaving themselves in church while their parents exchange greetings with others. While much of the conversation takes place in the church foyer, it carries over into the auditorium. Finding a seat is not difficult. Families sit in the same pew week after week unless ill health or the annual family vacation prevents them from doing so.

A few minutes before eleven, the pianist and organist begin playing. The auditorium becomes quieter as people prepare for worship. A few look over the order of service printed in their church bulletin and find the first hymn in their hymn book. Some are praying silently awaiting the beginning of the service. The worship service begins as the pastor makes his way to the pulpit and says, "Let's pray."

Following a brief prayer from the pastor, a prominent layman in the church makes his way to the pulpit. "Turn in your hymn book to hymn number thirty-seven, and let's stand to sing as we worship the Lord together," he announces. The people find the designated hymn as the organist begins playing the first verse. When the pianist joins on the last line, the lay songleader raises his arm and the congregation stands together.

With minor variations, this same service is being conducted in more than half the churches in America on any given Sunday morning. Different hymns will be chosen, but there are usually three or four in the course of the service. The last of these expresses some aspect of personal commitment to God and will be sung following the morning message by the pastor. Special music will take various forms. Sometimes the church choir will sing. On other occasions an adult member or group of members will sing. Occasionally, a group of children or young people will provide the special music.

Following the special music, the pastor returns to his pulpit. He thanks the person who has just sung for their "ministry in song this morning" and then reads the Scripture passage for that day. As he concludes the biblical passage, he invites the church to join him in praying for the needs of the church. The five-minute pastoral prayer mentions church concerns, members who are sick, and upcoming special events. The prayer is followed by announcements. People are encouraged to return for the evening service and reminded to attend Sunday school the next week. The announcements are usually followed by the offering. One of the ushers offers a brief prayer and the musicians play a hymn as the offering plate is passed.

Another hymn is sung just before the pastor comes to preach. In a larger congregational church, children are invited to attend a special church service called "children's church." In smaller churches, the children may gather at the front of the church for a special children's story by the pastor or some other member of the congregation. As the hymn concludes, people sit in their pews ready to listen to the sermon.

The emphasis of the pastor's sermon most Sunday mornings tends to be an exhortation based on a selected verse of Scripture or group of verses. The three points of the sermon tend to emphasize different aspects of the topic under consideration, perhaps each point suggesting a reason why the behavior advocated should be practiced. The people have come to identify the conclusion of the sermon by the extended story illustration or poem usually given by the pastor to end his message. As he completes the sermon, the pastor asks the congregation to stand as they sing together a hymn. Often the message of this closing hymn is related to the commitment he asked in the sermon.

As the hymn concludes, the pastor prays. In his brief prayer, he asks God to help them apply the message to their lives this week and watch over the church until they meet again. At the conclusion of the prayer, the pastor makes his way to the back of the auditorium as the musicians play another verse of the hymn. He greets each of the worshipers as they exit the auditorium. For some he has a special exhortation. The people gather their families to make their way home. Once again they have come together to worship God.

What Is the Purpose of the Congregational Church?

The last of the six worship styles considered in this book is the Congregational Church. These churches tend to be smaller than the other church types mentioned in this book, but their number may be greater than all other church types combined. Whereas the previous churches emphasized the leadership of the pastor as an evangelist, teacher, group leader, or worship leader, the Congregational Church emphasizes the people of the church because they are the congregation. Unlike other church types that are committed to a specific vision or mission of the church, congregational churches tend to have a more balanced commitment to various aspects of church ministries. This blended view of mission common among congregational churches is reflected in the following statement taken from a church constitution used by many of these churches: "The object of this church is set forth in its Covenant and Statement of Faith, namely: for worship, biblical instruction, the observance of the divinely instituted ordinances, the presentation of a corporate testimony to the power of the Gospel and its constituency and such service as the one supreme Lord and Lawgiver and taking His Word as its only and sufficient rule of faith and practice."

This view of the church and ministry also looks to the description of the church in the New Testament for its theological foundations. "The church is the Bride of Christ," explains one pastor, and "it is the goal of every bride to be a good W.I.F.E.," (the acrostic that represents Worship, Instruction, Fellowship, and Evangelism).

Worship is important in the Congregational Church, though its importance may not be as apparent as in a renewal congregation. The Sunday school/Sunday morning worship service combination often serves as the hub of all other ministries in the church. "Everyone who comes to Sunday school should stay for worship," explains one pastor. Predictably he adds, "And everyone coming for worship should get here early enough for Sunday School."

Christian education is also an important element of this church. In the past, this was largely accomplished through a closely graded Sunday school. Today, churches practice Christian education in a variety of forms. The educational ministries of a church may include discipleship training groups, home Bible studies, Training Union, Awana or Pioneer clubs for children, women's Bible study/coffee hour, and a host of similar offerings.

The Congregational Church likes to be perceived as a warm church where people can feel "at home." Coffee pots are apparent as people gather for Bible study. Fellowship times are planned to follow church services. Church suppers appear regularly on the church calendar. Usually these suppers are not catered. Rather, each family brings food that is shared with others during the meal.

Evangelism is also important to the Congregational Church. This church may not expect people to be saved every week, but it should happen periodically over the course of a year. Sometimes evangelism is tied to special church programs, such as an outreach Bible study, Vacation Bible School, or special youth meeting.

Balance is a key word describing the ministry of the Congregational Church. This church recognizes the same values as those identified by other worship styles but conscientiously strives not to emphasize one aspect of the ministry over another.

Expectations and Roles in the Congregational Church

The pastor has a unique role within the Congregational Church. Without question, he is a valued person in the minds of most church members, but he and his family are rarely allowed to become part of the church fellowship. Pastors exist in the Congregational Church to provide pastoral services. They are expected to conduct weddings and funerals, baptize converts, and preach sermons. It is assumed they will visit shut-ins and accept invitations to have dinner with various church families. Even when the relationship between pastor and parishioner is warm, there is distance.

It is not uncommon for congregational churches to recycle their pastors every two to three years. In the minds of church members, this is the norm. "Pastors come and go but laypeople build the church," explains one deacon in a congregational church. Church members expect to be involved in ministry. Indeed, pastors will find significant resistance in the church when he is perceived as doing too much. He probably works harder at more different things than pastors of noncongregational churches, but certain areas of ministry belong to the people. They expect to be involved in planning special events in the life of the church, such as church anniversaries and Christmas programs. And they expect everyone will have some role as these times are celebrated together.

The Bonding Agent of the Congregational Church

The Congregational Church differs from other worship styles in that there is no single glue that bonds members to one another. Rather, most congregational churches could be described as single-cell churches. Everyone knows everyone. Everyone relates to everyone. Everyone waits on everyone before anyone will do anything. Although a single-cell church can be stretched, the size of a congregational church is usually limited to the number of persons who can relate well to everyone else. Various church growth writers suggest a cell can grow to forty to sixty-six members. Beyond those limits, cells cease to function well.

The Congregational Church may be the most common worship style among American churches today. Statistical research suggests at least half of the churches in America are composed of fifty members or less. That percentage rises to about 75 percent when the upper limits of single-cell growth are considered. Most of these churches could probably be described as congregational churches.

Although there may be more congregational churches than other types, the size and nature of these churches hinders the rise of dominant leaders within the movement. In a single-cell church, the pastor who is a member of the church is often on the outside of the cell. Pastors often change every two or three years in a single-cell church. This constant change has little or no effect on the church's ongoing ministry. The strong lay involvement often hinders the emergence of strong pastoral leadership. "We were here before he came and we'll be here when he leaves," one layman explains. The church is happy to support their pastor in exchange for ministry received, but resists efforts to make significant changes to their ministry.

Even though there are no dominant leaders among congregational church-types, these churches are easily recognized. This is the church down the street or around the corner that looks very much like it looked fifteen years ago. It tends to experience an ongoing growth cycle with attendance ranging from forty to perhaps as high as a hundred worshipers. Most of the people attending the church are related to one another outside the church itself. In an older rural church, everyone in the church may be related to one another by blood or marriage. These other relationships shape the character of the church.

The Strengths and Contributions of the Congregational Church

The Congregational Church makes a significant contribution to church life in America, especially in the area of lay involvement. A member of one congregational church of only five families commented, "God has really blessed our church in that all our families tithe." The sacrificial giving of these five families was sufficient to enable this small church to maintain a church facility, pay a pastor's salary, and maintain the home in which his family lived. In some congregational churches, every member is involved in some ministry. Often, many members are involved in several ministries—perhaps too many.

The size of the Congregational Church is certainly a factor in the high membership involvement ratio characterizing these churches, but size alone is not a sufficient explanation for this phenomenon. Many members of congregational churches see their size as a hindrance to attracting new families to become involved. Congregational church members are involved in church ministries because they have bought into the vision of their church and taken ownership of the ministry. When this happens, people become increasingly involved in ministry, regardless of the size of the church.

A second strength of the Congregational Church is balance. True, many congregational churches are reluctant to try new ministries, but over the years these congregations have evolved a ministry that balances the worship of God with the study of His Word. These churches also balance outreach with inreach; they balance evangelistic ministries with ministries directed toward the members of the church itself.

While balance appears to have emerged without direction in many congregational churches, it has probably occurred because of the blend of giftedness within the church. Unlike other worship styles, this church is not tied to a single spiritual gift but rather includes members exercising all the spiritual gifts. Like the church at Corinth, they "come short in no gift" (1 Cor. 1:7). As each gifted member exercises his or her influence within the church, a balance emerges that makes room for all gifts. The example of the Congregational Church in this area stands as a challenge to other church types.

The Weaknesses of the Congregational Church

Despite these strengths, few congregational churches experience significant numerical growth. These growth limitations are directly tied to sociological factors that define the nature of this church type. So long as a congregational church remains tied to a single-cell church model, church growth will be limited to the maximum size of that cell (i.e., forty to sixty-six people). The Congregational Church may work hard to build attendance to a hundred or more, but without changing the infrastructure of their church, they will experience a decline in attendance. The key to increasing the size of a congregational church is to multiply cells.

In the early part of this century, Arthur Flake encouraged the growth of single-cell churches through a plan that multiplied cells within churches that tended to be congregational. His recommendations called for organizing their programs for outreach, enlisting workers, providing adequate facilities for growth, taking a neighborhood census to find and enlist prospects, providing good Bible teaching and preaching, visiting prospects and absentees, and attempting to involve everyone in the total program of the church. Adherence to these principles has resulted in the significant growth of the Southern Baptist Convention in the twentieth century. Flake was so convinced his program would work he claimed, "Development in Sunday School growth is not confined to any particular locality or section of the country nor to any special types of Sunday schools. Rural churches, town churches, and city churches, both in 'downtown' and residential sections, can experience a material increase in enrollment and in attendance when right methods of Sunday School building are employed."[1]

Tapping into the Strength of the Congregational Church

If the strength of the Congregational Church is people participating in ministry, all churches can tap into its strength by returning ministry to the people. In the pursuit of excellence in ministry, there has been a gradual shift in American churches from lay involvement to professional expertise in conducting ministry. This is widely perceived as necessary in some circles if the church is indeed going to achieve its goal of serving God with excellence.

How can a church achieve greater lay participation in ministry yet maintain a high level of excellence in the quality of church ministry? By using a gift-based strategy for enlisting workers for ministry. People who use their spiritual gifts in ministry are usually highly motivated and strive to do a much better job than otherwise expected. Indeed, excellence in ministry can be enhanced by enlisting gifted laypersons to serve in their areas of expertise.

In the past, enlisting workers tended to follow a certain pattern. First there was the list of jobs to be filled. Then there was the list of willing workers, or those who could be talked into being willing under the right circumstances. Young couples became youth sponsors because they could relate to the youth. Mothers with young children were perceived to be the best nursery workers. The oldest deacon taught the adult Bible class.

A gift-based enlistment strategy begins with the worker, then moves to ministry opportunities. Those who are gifted in evangelism are challenged to consider involvement in evangelistic ministries. Gifted shepherds are asked to consider leading Sunday school classes or small groups. Mercy-showers are scattered throughout ministries to young children and seniors as well as shut-in and hospital visitation. Each person is given the opportunity to serve God in the areas in which God has uniquely gifted them.

Under the old approach to enlistment, workers tended to serve out of a sense of duty and were often motivated by guilt. They worked hard to ensure the job was done, but their hearts were not always in ministry, and some did not find personal fulfillment in their accomplishments. With the new approach to ministry, people serve God with the realization they are using the unique gifts He has given them to accomplish what He wants them doing. As they see God accomplish things through their efforts, they sense personal fulfillment that continues to motivate them in ministry. Pastors using a gift-based approach to ministry find people remain involved in ministry longer than under the previous system.

What is the downside to gift-based ministry? First, some jobs may go unfilled. Perhaps this is because it is unnecessary. One church failed to find members for a church committee for two consecutive years. Consequently, church leaders decided the committee had outlived its function.

Second, a gifted member may hide out in the church. As church members begin to understand the role of spiritual gifts in ministry, they will become more interested in discovering, developing, and using their spiritual gifts in ministry. A spiritual gift seminar or series of messages on different gifts by the pastor is often effective in helping Christians discover their spiritual gift and begin moving into significant ministries where they can serve God.

As long as there have been people of God, there has been a congregational church. Sometimes it is called the informal church or the "low church," in contrast to the more formal liturgical or "high church." The Congregational Church has been made up of Pilgrims, Puritans, Brethren, and Mennonites. It has been called the Free Church in Scandinavia, the Anabaptist in the Netherlands, the Dissenters in England, and the Huguenots in France. The Congregational Church is simply the church of the people, by the people, and for the people. It is the people's church where they love God, serve God, and worship God. And since God indwells the people, a congregational church is God's church.

PART THREE

Principles to Remember

CHAPTER ELEVEN

Nineteen Observations and Five Suggestions to Help Prevent a Worship War in Your Church

Worship is God's tool to restore order, establish beauty, and help people find meaning in their lives.

Christians worship differently. That's because we are different: different mixtures of spiritual gifts, different callings, different personalities, different backgrounds, and different doctrine. We also have different methods of teaching and different ways to express worship. Our differences produce as many different individual responses to worship as there are different expressions of worship. And the intensity of people's response to our differences in worship is as deep as the differences among people.

Worship Eyes

Some have *wide-open* worship eyes to see the various ways that people worship the Triune God. They rejoice in the diversity of worship as much as they rejoice in worship itself. They shout praises with the Renewal Church, they study the Word of God in the Bible Expositional Church, and they are quietly respectful in the Liturgical Church.

Others have *clouded* worship eyes. They tolerate the differences in worship expression. While they would never shout "Hallelujahs," they conclude, "It's alright for them, but that's not my style." Some from the soul-winning Evangelistic Church will not criticize the quiet Liturgical Church but will tolerate them as long as their commitment to doctrinal purity remains true. Clouded eyes say, "Live and let live."

Some have *blinded* worship eyes. They criticize those who are different. They criticize others for several reasons: (1) others compromise Scripture, (2) others neglect Scripture, (3) others misinterpret Scripture, or (4) others wrongly apply Scripture. This critical group is not saying those different from them are un-Christian or disobedient to Christ. They are not calling others heretics or cults; they are just critical of the way others worship God.

A last group has *hardened* worship eyes toward differences in worship. This last group sharply criticizes those who disagree with them. They claim that those who worship differently from them are wrong. Over the years, I have heard representatives from just about every worship expression claim, "My way of worship is the best way because . . ." And they give biblical argument to prove their scriptural method of worship. But their criticism of others usually goes a second mile. They attack others with the claim, "My way of worship is the only way because . . ."

The critical group usually attacks others for being unbiblical or antibiblical. They defend their way of worship as the method demanded by God. (But remember: God does not demand a type of worship; He wants the fact of worship.) This group usually attacks others because they are forced by the totalitarian focus of their exclusive methodology to negate anything that is different from them.

Nineteen Observations about Worship

The following observations will help you interpret the various expressions of worship and put controversy in perspective. Though they do not apply to all situations, they can guide you through the maze of "worship wars" and help you to understand what is happening in the world.

Observation 1: Some worshipers probably have the same worship experience, even though they express themselves with different forms. The validity of biblical worship is not measured by the outward form of worship. Biblical worship is valid when one worships God in spirit (total expression from the heart) and truth (according to the truth of God in Scriptures). If outward sincerity were the only true measurement, those who sincerely bring their rice offering to Buddha, praying with weeping and anguish, may be just as effective as the Christian. But worshiping Buddha is not biblical. The legitimacy of worship is measured by one's relationship to God through Christ, not the sincerity of the worshiper.

Observation 2: Worship is legitimate when God is its focus. "What did God get out of the worship service?" may be a legitimate question. When God is worshiped in spirit, then God is magnified, glorified, and exalted. Technically, God cannot be magnified, because the word *magnify* means "to get larger" or "to grow in intensity." God does not change; He is immutable. So in that sense, no worshiper can make God greater than what He is, nor can God grow to something beyond His present nature. To magnify God is similar to one who uses eyeglasses to magnify the print on the page. Newsprint does not become larger, the print becomes larger in the perception of the reader. So when God is magnified, He becomes larger in our perception; as a result we are transformed and we live differently.

Worship is ascribing to God the worth that is due to Him. When God is magnified or glorified, He is getting the glory that He deserves because of who He is, and He is lifted up in the adoration of His people because of what He has done.

Worshipers in a rural Georgia church may express their high regard for God by shouting "Hallelujah" and punctuating the sermons with "Amen." Worshipers may express gratitude to God when the southern quartet sings, "I've Got a Mansion Just over the Hilltop." The worshipers know their home in heaven is so much greater than their home on earth. They magnify the Lord for His provision. That act of worship can be just as uplifting as that of the British, who enter the cathedral and kneel in prayer as the sunlight streams through the stained-glass window.

Observation 3: Expressions of worship are not hierarchical, but express a range of emotions and understanding in the heart of the worshiper. The term *hierarchical* implies an organization of rank—each subordinates to the one above. Those who rank the types of worship say that the first is the best, or reconsidering the perspective, they might say that the last is best. Some think the "twang" of a guitar and the southern gospel quartet on Sunday morning is "corny" or superficial because it reflects a type of culture they think is less civilized than the culture of Bach and Handel. They think the operatic voice is purer than the popular voice and exalts God in a high way. But the quality of one's voice is measured by the hearer. Some think the best opera is the Grand Ole Opry. One's perception of quality does not determine the legitimacy of worship. Also included is skill, understanding of music, type of music, and expression of art form.

Therefore, there is no hierarchy in quality expressions of worship, and one is not better than another, nor does worship become more effective as one moves across the six paradigms.

Some claim their form of worship is better because the church experiences the numerical growth of worshipers, the life of the worshiper becomes more holy, or some other form of empirical measurement; therefore, the worship experience is better because its results are better.

Still others claim that worship must express a type or system of biblical doctrine. Hence, they apply a theological standard to establish a hierarchy of worship. Just because one can connect his worship experience with proper biblical terminology does not necessarily mean that the worship experience is deeper or richer or more biblical. The person of Jesus Christ can be just as real to the worshiper in the Renewal Church as He is to the worshiper in the Congregational Church. One's system of theology and knowledge of theology may or may not determine the rank of worship to the worshiper or to God. The hierarchical question is not one of doctrinal purity, but the issue is the experiential indwelling presence of Jesus Christ in a person's life. Does Jesus dwell in the life of the worshiper? Does the worshiper magnify the Lord Jesus Christ with life and lips? Is God being magnified with this person's worship?

However, doctrinal elasticity has its limits. There is a point of no return beyond which God can or cannot bless and beyond which the person of Jesus Christ will or will not indwell a person. This is the essential or fundamentals of the faith. Just as one cannot take away the essentials of an automobile and still have an automobile that functions, so a person cannot take away the essential truths of Christianity and still have valid faith. Those who deny the essentials of Christianity, or are ignorant of them, cannot worship God in any valid way. Each person must examine his own doctrine and experience in light of Scripture.

The question becomes one of personal perspective. I should not measure the worship of others to determine how close they are to God, or how close they are to me, or even if I think they are worshiping correctly. I should be concerned with my own spiritual growth. Is Christ real to me? Am I magnifying God in my worship? How can I get closer to Him?

Observation 4: The strengths that characterize each worship expression are also found in the other expressions. Those who worship God in the Evangelistic Church tend to think they are the most effective soul-winners because they may have an evangelistic outreach visitation program every week, or they may have soul-winning training for their laypeople, and the sermons end with the gospel invitation where people may be invited to come forward to pray to receive Christ. Some in the Evangelistic Church tend to think that other churches are less spiritual because those churches do not focus on soul-winning. The problem with this attitude is that they elevate themselves by minimizing the contribution of others or even negate the contribution of others.

Just as no man is an island to himself, no worship expression has an exclusive handle on its strength. As an illustration, if a church sings the content of the gospel, preaches the Word of God, and honestly prays, it will have some evangelistic outreach. While evangelistic outreach may not be the primary factor in a specific church, it does not mean that there is no evangelism in that church. Wherever the Word of God is communicated to the hearts of unsaved people, the lost can see their sin, understand that Jesus died for their sin, and accept God's forgiveness in His Son Jesus Christ. This is true whether it is in a Bible expositional message, a renewal message of motivation, or in the devotional sermon of the Liturgical Church.

Each of the six worship styles makes its own dominant contribution to worshipers, and to some degree or another, the qualities of that contribution are found in the other churches.

- The Evangelistic Church: getting people saved
- The Bible Expositional Church: teaching people the Word of God
- The Renewal Church: motivating people to holiness and obedience
- The Body Life Church: helping people find meaning through significant relationships
- The Liturgical Church: magnifying God in atmospheric worship
- The Congregational Church: involving members in the local body of Christ

As we view the six contributions of the six worship styles, we recognize that the main contribution of each is also found in the other five worship forms. Probably all New Testament churches have some manifestation of these strengths somewhere in their life and ministry.

The question is not what church is right or which church is better. The question is this: Which church best meets your need and best helps you express your worship to God?

Observation 5: No single worship expression has a corner on the market to the exclusion of the other worship expressions. The problem with this view is that people worship God differently in Scripture. Isaiah saw the Lord high and lifted up, and he was broken: "Woe is me" (Isa. 6:5). God met Jeremiah and had to build up the timid prophet's self-esteem (Jer. 1:4–10). Paul was blinded and fell at the feet of Jesus (Acts 9:4–5). Solomon stood in the temple (2 Chron. 6:12). David sat in the tabernacle (2 Sam. 7:18). John fell on his face (Rev. 1:17). The church elders knelt (Acts 20:36). The Bible doesn't tell us how to worship but exhorts us to worship with our hearts, hands, voices and minds. We are to worship with our total prayers, confession of sin, Scripture, affirmation of our faith, and the like.

Obviously, I do not think that any one worship paradigm is the only valid expression or that any one is better than another. They all express aspects of biblical methods or means. In some cultures, a certain worship paradigm may express worship for a certain group of people better than another. Throughout history, some worship paradigms have been more effective at some times than at others.

Observation 6: Various reflections of worship may be characteristic of different times in a person's life. Most people go through phases of life when they express their Christianity differently than at other times. There may be times when we spend more time in the Word of God; at other times we spend more time in prayer; and still at other times we feel a need to sing hymns and worship God. This recognizes the fact that we have changing needs—we grow in our understanding, as well as develop our emotional response to life. Because we have different spiritual needs, we will take advantage of different ministries from God to help us meet those needs. At times we need to reach out in obedience to the Great Command: to love our neighbor as we love ourself. At this time, the body life service may reflect our spiritual need better than anything else, so we grow in that type of church. Later, when we feel lethargy in our growth, we may need the excitement of the Renewal Church. Still later in life, as we become more mature in our understanding, we want to become more involved in the life of our local church, so we move toward the Congregational Church form of worship.

Let us be careful about telling others that their experience is wrong or less effective because it is different from ours. It may be that God is using a certain experience to minister to a person in a certain time in his life. Later, he may have a different need and express his Christian worship differently.

Observation 7: Worship experiences have become standardized in churches because people with similar needs gravitate toward one another, colonizing together to meet their needs. Those with the gift of teaching tend to go to a Bible expositional church, and those with the spiritual gift of evangelization go to an evangelistic church. The same thing happens with the gift of exhortation: those with that gift attend a renewal church. Those with the gift of mercy-showing might go to a church where their leader is a mercy-shower (i.e., a facilitator of *koinonia*); and their need of relationship is reciprocally given to others and accepted from them. They attend a Body Life Church. This does not mean that one church is better than another; it means that one church has a different ministry to the different needs of individuals; perhaps in different phases of their lives.

However, this does not mean that experience is everything and doctrine is secondary. All experience must be grounded in objective doctrine. But remember, many in one church with the same experience will tend to support others in their church and seek to verify their experience by Scripture. Once they have verified their worship experience, they classify it and then make it the standard for all others. As a result, both their doctrine and their worship experience become the predominant theme of their church. They claim that doctrine is now the foundation of their worship and worship is the expression of their doctrine, but many times neither is true. Instead of exegesis (interpreting from the Scriptures what is there), they're guilty of isogesis (reading into the Scriptures what they want it to mean).

Observation 8: Churches from the same denomination may be found in all six worship experiences. As I have traveled the churches of America, I have been amazed at the types of worship I have seen in some denominations. Many times people think that Southern Baptist churches are homogeneous in nature; that is, all their pastors preach a three-point evangelistic sermon, followed by a gospel invitation. This is not so. Southern Baptist churches reflect each of the six worship expressions. However, in my opinion, most Southern Baptist churches are found in the congregational worship style. On the other hand, some would think that all Presbyterian churches are liturgical in worship style. Again, this is not true. Many Presbyterian ministers who have graduated from Dallas Theological Seminary mold their worship services around Bible expositional sermons. Their churches have become teaching centers of the Word of God, with a lesser commitment to liturgical expressions of worship.

Observation 9: There is a correlation between experience and doctrine even though it is difficult to see a cause-and-effect relationship. In the summer of 1960 I was the executive secretary of the Greater Saint Louis Sunday School Association. One of my requirements was to visit all of the cooperating churches to organize the National Sunday School Association Convention to be held in October of that year. I visited and spoke in many Pentecostal churches. I had preconceptions about what went on in Assembly of God, Church of God, Pentecostal Holiness, and other pentecostal-type churches. My preconception was based on a bias that was reinforced by my Presbyterian roots and a few Pentecostals I had met in an interdenominational Bible college. However, that summer I experienced some Pentecostal churches with high church liturgical services. I remember thinking, *They're just like Presbyterians.* Over the years I have concluded that you will find all six worship expressions in churches holding pentecostal doctrine. That summer I changed my view of those churches that are holiness or pentecostal in doctrine and lifestyle. I came to love them and appreciate them as I do all who belong to Christ.

Therefore, I have come to believe that there is not a cause-and-effect relationship between church doctrine and church worship. Not all churches in any denomination or with a theological tradition will follow an expected worship model. However, there may be a correlation, hence more charismatic churches would use renewal worship than most other worship forms.

There has usually been a relationship between what a church taught and what it practiced in worship. By this I mean that most mainline denominational high churches gravitated to a liturgical expression of worship. Also, most Baptist churches gravitated to a congregational type of worship.

Historically, churches with deeper commitment to doctrine have tended toward less outward emotional experiences in their worship. These churches tend to emphasize thinking, rationality, insight, and acting on what is known. On the other hand, those churches that have a deeper commitment to experiential Christianity, such as found in Holiness, soul-winning, and Pentecostal churches, have tended to gravitate toward worship experiences that reflected feeling, sensitivity, and intuitive experience. When this happens, it is difficult to determine if Scripture is used to verify experience, or if experience is verified by Scripture. However, both become foundational to the church's mission.

Observation 10: No one type of worship service meets all the needs of all of its members. The seeker service may meet evangelistic needs, but people may leave not having felt the presence of the Lord. Also, contemporary worship may get people involved in worshipful expressions, but they go away hungry because they were not fed the Word of God.

Observation 11: Some believers begin at one experience and gravitate throughout life from one worship experience to another. While this process is not a scriptural exhortation, nor is it normative, it may represent some Christians who are caught up in experientialism and experimentation. When a believer gravitates from one worship experience to another, it is not necessarily growth in grace, but it is growth in experience.

It is probably not healthy for a person to continually change his worship experience. However, when a new worship experience makes Christ more real in his life, I am not against changing one's worship experience. But when a person is motivated by love, it is easy to see how he constantly goes deeper in his perspective, switching from one worship experience to another. A person may begin in the Evangelistic Church; then sensing his shallowness of doctrine, he may gravitate to the Bible Expositional Church. Next, sensing a shallowness of feeling, maybe he will gravitate to the Renewal Church. As his love is renewed, he feels a desire for closer harmony with other believers, hence he may gravitate to the Body Life Church. This person, always wanting to go deeper, may then begin looking for the next experience and find a deeper warmth with God in the Liturgical Church, whereby in silence, meditation, and deep awe, he can worship God. Could this person finally end up in the Congregational Church, becoming completely involved in the local body of Christ? The Bible calls this type of person immature—"children, tossed to and fro" (Eph. 4:14).

Let's be slow to criticize those who change their worship experience. Christ may become more real to them, even though their experience reflects some aspects of emotional immaturity.

Observation 12: Some worshipers are converted within one worship experience and remain there throughout their lives. Those who open their heart to God and the teaching of their church usually have the type of conversion experience that is suggested or expected by their church. Those who are converted in renewal churches tend to have a deeply emotional conversion experience. Those attending a Bible expositional church tend to be converted as they understand the propositional truths of Scripture and respond with full intellectual belief.

Because a person is yielded to God and responds to the message that is preached from his local church pulpit, he does not seek alternate experiences from other churches or from other sources. This person remains within the framework of his home church (even though he may change churches, he will seek another that has the same worship style); hence, he remains within one worship experience for his entire Christian life. This is probably the history of most worshipers. When they find any internal yearning to change their worship experience, they may interpret their feeling as a temptation and reject it. They tend to remain true to the doctrine and worship style of their church. They tend to have a relatively solid experiential foundation for their Christian life, and they live and die in the faith in which they were first born again.

Observation 13: When worshipers move geographically, it is best for them to seek a church that will maximize their strengths. There comes a time when we leave our church because our jobs move us, we retire, or because of many other valid reasons. When we leave the worship experience we've had all our lives, we are faced with choosing another worship experience. You should be careful of choosing a worship style that is novel, unusual, or just different for the sake of being different.

Know your spiritual gifts, and choose a church that will maximize your spiritual usefulness to God. Just as we instruct a Sunday school staff to use people where they are useable, so we would instruct those moving from one church to another to choose a church that can maximize their strengths.

Observation 14: When God puts believers in a worship experience that has different expectations than their giftedness, it's better for them to recognize what they can do than complain about what they cannot do. Sometimes a person will find himself in a church that is different from the method of worship that he has experienced, yet it will be difficult to change churches because other churches are not available. This could be a situation for a military family, a person who is on a temporary business assignment, or a person who is in a neighborhood where there is only one church.

When you find yourself in a body of believers that worships differently than your strengths, begin by knowing yourself. You may worship in a typical Baptist congregational church, but you really desire a renewal or a Bible expositional church. Rather than complaining about the present church, submit yourself to the congregation. Also, rather than trying to change their worship style, recognize what you can do; then use your strengths and gifts in the church to accomplish the glory of God.

A person with strong teaching gifts may feel comfortable in a Bible expositional church, but finds himself in an evangelistic church. He should invest his teaching gifts to train as many as possible in the Word of God. The Lord would probably tell the person with dominant skills, "Bloom where you are planted."

Observation 15: Since different methods of Christian worship present problems to some people, we should not emphasize our differences but the unity we have in Jesus Christ. Even though we may use different expressions of worship, we still worship the same God from the depths of our hearts. "There is one body and one Spirit, just as you were called in one hope of your calling; one Lord, one faith, one baptism; one God and Father of all, who is above all, and through all, and in you all" (Eph. 4:6).

Following this same theme, Jesus prayed, "That they all may be one" (John 17:21). While He prayed for unity among Christians—which is a heart attitude of accepting one another as Christ accepted them—this unity does not mean union. Union means all believers must join the same denomination and do things the same way. Union is everyone doing the same thing, in the same way, at the same time, because we have to.

The secret of our unity is, "I in them, and thou in me, that they may be made perfect in one" (John 17:23, KJV). Because Christ is in us, He is a common object of our love and worship. We are one in Christ. That does not mean we unite in relationship to do or give the same identical worship expression. We can come to the worship experience with a unity of love, commitment, and desire to magnify God.

Observation 16: Even though some express their worship differently than we do, we are not obligated to follow their methods of worship. A method of worship, like all methods used in the church, is defined as "the application of principle to culture." By this definition, our methods will change because culture changes from age to age. This does not mean we change our doctrine, nor does it mean we change our principles. It means that we take eternal truth (our doctrine) and apply the Word of God to minister to people where they are (in culture) so that they may worship God effectively.

The content of our doctrine is not negotiable. (My purpose for writing this book is not to ask believers to change their doctrine.) Also, principles are eternal. The principles of praying, teaching, evangelism, and holiness cannot change. But what changes? Our methods change with time, and our methods change in culture.

What are some changes in worship methods? Some people worship God with a guitar. When I first became a youth minister, guitars were primarily identified with youth and the counterculture movement; so none brought a guitar into our church—at least into most Baptist churches I identified with. Guitars had always been used in Pentecostal and Holiness churches, in Salvation Army citadels, as well as in minority churches where guitars were the dominant instrument of choice. The very fact that certain minorities used guitars indicates that the use of guitars was a method, not an eternal principle; it had nothing to do with doctrine. The same could be said for the use of candles, hymnbooks as opposed to psalters, or an acoustical piano as opposed to an electronic piano. These are cultural choices that fall in the realm of methods. They have nothing to do with principles and/or doctrine.

Observation 17: Because most Christians want to keep the worship traditions that make their church unique, they fight change because it is unsettling. Most Christians strive to remain faithful to God by remaining faithful to their experiences when God first touched them. They think by allegiance to their experiences (that grow out of doctrine), they are also being faithful to the purity of doctrine. Since the Bible says much about not changing doctrine, they view the change in worship expression with the same reservation.

The New Testament exhorts us to be faithful to doctrine—"Those things which are most surely believed among us" (Luke 1:1, KJV). Christian truth is quite often known as "sound doctrine." Paul notes, "Holding fast the faithful word as he has been taught, that he may be able, by sound doctrine, both to exhort and to convict those who contradict" (Titus 1:9).

And why do Christians fight over the differences in worship expression? Obviously, the exhortation to defend sound doctrine is connected to defending worship that is attached to doctrine. "I gave all diligence to write unto you of the common salvation . . . and exhort you that ye should earnestly contend for the faith which was once delivered unto the saints" (Jude 3, KJV). After we begin contending for doctrine, it is easy to contend for one's worship style. Those who contend for a worship style think anyone who denies true doctrine is to be rejected. "Whoever transgresses and does not abide in the doctrine of Christ does not have God. He who abides in the doctrine of Christ has both the Father and the Son" (2 John 9). "Whoever denies the Son does not have the Father either" (1 John 2:23). Therefore, anyone who denies the fundamental doctrine of Christ is to be rejected.

Observation 18: We should be wary of the elitist who rejects worship that is different from his or her own expression. An elitist usually views his life and works as far superior to others, and some elitists see their worship as better than others. This becomes a dangerous practice, for the elitist introduces the temptation to (1) judge, (2) set oneself over another, (3) be prideful, and (4) despise another brother. The very elitist who would elevate himself into the heart of God usually blinds himself to the presence of God because he has succumbed to the sin of a pharisaical attitude by "think [ing] himself to be something" (Gal. 6:3, KJV).

Observation 19: Most worship wars break out because leaders have not taught people how to worship, when to worship, and why to worship. When we better educate people about worship, everyone can worship in a more meaningful way. Also, most will be more tolerant one of another.

Leaders should keep the worship experience elevated so that the non-church attenders may appreciate and understand the dynamics of what is happening. I am not sure that we should plan Sunday morning for only the unchurched, nor should we have a worship service that excludes the unsaved. A service for both has been called "the blended service."

We should be sensitive to the unchurched and help them enter with the proper attitude and focus. Specifically, the unsaved should realize that worship will not save them. However, God does not reject the "worthship due Him" from unsaved church attenders. When the psalmist cried, "Make a joyful noise unto the LORD, all ye lands" (Ps. 100:1, KJV), he was commanding the unsaved nations (Gentiles) outside Israel to worship God. Also, in the final Judgment Day the unsaved will worship God, but then it will be too late to be converted. But nevertheless, "Every tongue should confess that Jesus Christ is Lord, to the glory of God the Father" (Phil. 2:11).

Everyone must worship; it is not an option. Worship must come from our heart and must be consistent with Scripture. However, there is a choice in worship—a choice of how we will tell God we love Him.

Five Suggestions to Help Prevent a Worship War in Your Church

After making several observations about the six worship expressions, there is another step that needs our attention. Here are five suggestions every person must follow:

Suggestion 1: Learn tolerance. Because of the biblical nature of each of the six worship expressions, all worshipers ought to be tolerant of those who apply New Testament worship differently. If in fact they are worshiping God the Father according to the Scriptures—and they are worshiping Him with all their hearts—they are not disobedient believers. We must all recognize the biblical basis for each worship paradigm.

Suggestion 2: Strive for balance in the body of Christ. When a church emphasizes a certain strength in worship expression, it should also recognize its weakness. When a congregation overemphasizes one worship expression, it is probably de-emphasizing strengths found in other churches. There is strength in every weakness and in every weakness there is strength. When we see our weaknesses in the mirror of our strengths, we should strive for a well-rounded local body of Christ that reflects all spiritual gifts.

Ideally, all churches should be well-rounded, which is another way of saying all churches should be similar. But that is not the case. We live in a world made up of different people, from different ethnocentric minorities, with different perspectives on life. While there is a homogeneity in human nature and personality, the cultural differences drive us to diversity. Therefore, we should all strive for a well-balanced worship service that involves all believers, and all of their spiritual gifts, so that everyone gives the "worthship" to God that is due to Him. However, the diversity of individuals accounts for the many expressions of worship. When all people worship God from their hearts, and in the comfort of their cultural expressions, God can touch them and direct their lives.

Suggestion 3: Recognize the strengths of the church where you found Christ, and what that church has contributed to your view of Christianity. Almost everyone remembers the church and the worship service where they were saved. Also, the place where they were grounded in their faith will always have an enduring influence in their perspective. Since you can't rewrite history and you can't undo experiences, you have to grow according to the roots that have been planted in the soil. Therefore, know yourself, know your background, and worship the way you have to worship.

Suggestion 4: Discover your spiritual gifts and worship from your strengths. Part of worshiping properly is to know your spiritual gifts. Because many churches represent a colony of spiritual giftedness, you ought to know both your dominant spiritual gift and the dominant gift in the church where you are attending. This will help you maximize your strengths to the church, and it will help you understand what contribution the church will make to your maturity and growth in grace.

Suggestion 5: Realize how the church contributes to you if its dominant spiritual gift is different from yours. When God leads you to a church that has a worship expression that is different from your expectation, you should not fight it nor try to split the church or even lead people out of the church. Try to learn what you can about the church and grow in grace. Then recognize how you can make your best contribution to that church. If it is an evangelistic church and your gift is Bible teaching, don't push for sermons that are solely Bible teaching oriented. Try to determine how you can use your spiritual gift of teaching to strengthen the church in which God has placed you.

CHAPTER TWELVE

The Future of Worship

These people make a big show of saying the right thing,
But their heart isn't in it.
They act like they are worshiping me,
But they don't mean it.
They just use me as a cover,
For teaching whatever suits their fancy.
Ditching God's command,
And taking up the latest fads.

Mark 7:6–7, The Message

The core of worship can never change. God will always seek worship (John 4:24), and there will always be a centrifugal force drawing people to God, so there will always be a yearning in the heart to worship God. As long as people live on the earth there will be worshipers of God, and as long as people live in the limited body called flesh, we will never perfectly worship God.

Our thinking is not accurate.

Our response is not perfect.

Our love of God is not complete.

Our godly desires are not without flaw.

As a result . . .

Worship will be reflected in different ways.

Worship music will be sung to different tempos.

Worship voices will be lifted in different harmonies.

Worship hands will be joined in different expressions.

Worship buildings will have a different feel.

When I speak of the future of worship, I am not trying to predict what will happen in the future, nor am I predicting a new expression of worship to join the six expressions I've described in this book. Trying to predict the future of worship is like predicting where lightning will strike and what pattern it will make the next time it strikes. Both lightning and worship are dynamic, energetic, and powerful—flashing brilliance from one pole to another. Lightning flashes in an electrically charged cloud to a receptive condition on earth. Worship flashes between God and His people—finite humans giving to God the worthship that is due to the infinite Creator and Owner of the universe. And in the act of worship, men and women receive power and energy to carry on His life on planet earth.

Recent Trends in Worship

I have witnessed the following trends in worship since World War II.

Christians are experiencing a growing thirst for God. There seems to be a desire to know God—not to know about Him, but to know Him. More and more people want to bless God—not just to get Him to bless them. He seems to be the growing focus of more and more Christians. They are carrying out the passion of Paul, "That I may know Him, and the power of His resurrection" (Phil. 3:10).

Christians are experiencing a growing thirst for worship. There seems to be a growing hunger on the part of Christians to encounter God and revel in His presence. More than the Renewal Church or Liturgical Church, God's people crave a real divine encounter.

Obviously, attendance is up at the worship services of evangelical churches. At the same time Sunday schools, fellowship hours, evangelistic crusades, or the many other meetings conducted by the church are declining in attendance.

Worship has an awe that attracts worshipers. It has mystery that intrigues those who don't know God. It has passion that many empty-hearted people need. Attendance at worship services has grown because of what you become. Worship has some teaching, as does Sunday school, but Sunday school is declining. Worship has fellowship as other organizations offer fellowship, but they are not effective. Worship is growing while others are not because, in worship alone, the created human mirrors God in whose image he or she was created.

Christians are allowing increasing spontaneity in worship. Worship is more spontaneous in America today than it has been in many years. Some of this spontaneity is being driven by culture where Americans become more responsive to television, video games, and life in general. Another driving force of spontaneity is new expectations in worship. Pastors expect people to become more involved than ever before. The term *user-friendly* means bringing the person into the market and the market into the person—the key phrase for both Bible teaching and worship.

The worship service is no longer a well-designed sequence of events that is controlled by the pastor. More often than not, the audience is given opportunity to respond, read, lift hands, share, or actively pray.

The Holy Spirit is inspiring and releasing wholehearted worship in people of all expressions. Whether you attend a renewal church, a liturgical church, or even a congregational church, the Holy Spirit seems to be working in people today as they become involved in worship services.

For years pastors have prayed for the anointing of the Holy Spirit and/or the filling of the Holy Spirit. Whether they are looking for atmospheric worship, atmospheric revival, or just an answer to God's promise, "I will pour out My spirit upon all flesh," they are seeking the presence of the Holy Spirit in their worship services. In response, most churches today have a more vibrant worship because believers are allowing the Holy Spirit to work through them.

There is a growing emphasis on the work of the Holy Spirit. This growing emphasis has come from several sources. First is the influence of pentecostalism, also named the First Wave. It brought a focus of the Holy Spirit in the life of the believer. The Second Wave brought tongues into many churches; that is, nonpentecostal churches developed a charismatic expression of prayer language. This Second Wave focused the attention of the evangelical world on the Holy Spirit. The Third Wave describes the growth of power evangelism, a manifestation of "signs and wonders" in certain churches. This also brings attention to the Holy Spirit.

Before the charismatic/pentecostal phenomena brought new focus on the Holy Spirit, for years dispensationalist Bible teachers have called the Church Age the Age of the Holy Spirit. They have focused on the ministry of the Holy Spirit in the study of Scriptures. Then beginning in the sixties and seventies there was a growth of attention on spiritual gifts, spiritual gift inventories, and preaching to help people find their spiritual gifts; this attention is found in both charismatic and noncharismatic churches, and has brought the Holy Spirit into new attention and to new focus in many churches.

Since "no one can say that Jesus is Lord except by the Holy Spirit" (1 Cor. 12:3), we see a growing influence of the Holy Spirit in all types of worship services.

Worship is becoming more a celebration than a program. Whereas in the past, many have looked at worship as a "service," worship is becoming a free-flowing celebration that involves healing, understanding, and a commitment of the will. People are clapping, shouting, lifting hands, singing contemporary songs of praise. And judging from the view on their faces, they seem to be enjoying it more.

Worship is flowing from the total person: intellect, emotion, and will. It flows from spirit, soul, and body (1 Thess. 5:23). The Christian must "love the Lord your God with all your heart, with all your soul, with all your mind, and with all your strength" (Mark 12:30). And how do we love God, but to worship Him involving all of these abilities of ours? It seems that as people know more about worship, they feel deeper about worship, and they are responding in decisive acts of the will.

Worship is becoming more demonstrative. While this point has been noted in previous observations, people are largely becoming more expressive in their worship. More churches are adding "kneelers" at the altar— not just liturgical churches. People are asked to bow, making it a decisive act of their will; people are asked to lift hands or to clap in a show of appreciation. Whether you agree with the expression, "Let's give Jesus a hand," it is a response to the biblical admonition to "clap your hands" (Ps. 47:1). To these demonstrative acts add shouting, praising God; and to these even add prayer excursion, prayer journeys, and prayer walking. Whatever the response, these are expressions that reflect the depth of worship that many Christians are now feeling.

The atmospheric presence of God is increasingly felt in worship. Many have used the phrases *atmospheric revival* and *atmospheric worship* to describe that which was "felt" in a particular meeting of Christians. Whereas revival is defined "God pouring Himself out on His people," atmospheric revival occurs when people feel the presence of God. Atmospheric worship implies the successful worship of God so that He comes as the object of worship and receives worship that is directed to Him; hence people feel His presence.

Psalm 22:3 is often used to describe this phenomenon, "Oh, thou that inhabitest the praises of Israel" (KJV), meaning God lives in the praises of His people. Since that is so, then people can produce atmospheric worship by praising God, because God's presence will come into the presence of His people when He is praised.

People have always believed in the omnipresence of God—that God is always present equally, at all places, at all times. Add to this the transcendence of God—that He is high and sovereign, He is beyond all of us, for God dwelleth in the heavens. But to this add the imminence that He is always close to every one of us. In the atmosphere of worship, He who is close to us is worshiped, even though He is the sovereign Lord of the universe. In the act of worship we bring the sovereign Lord into our presence so we can feel His presence.

Changes in Church Life

The changes in the way the church is organized and conducted will make changes in worship. And the changes of society and culture will change the church because the church must reach out to touch and change culture. And in the process of taking its place in culture and incorporating the people into its membership, the church will be influenced by culture.

Multiuse Buildings

In the past the church sanctuary was a sacred place, and the colonists built their church before constructing any other community building. But the day of the restricted sanctuary is passing. The cost of property and construction has forced the church to use multiuse facilities, thus creating the sanctitorium (sanctuary and auditorium) and the gymnatorium (gym and auditorium).

Multiservices

Because of zoning laws, parking restrictions, and financial limitations, many churches have added multiservices to use the sanctuary and parking area more than once. Ward Presbyterian Church, Livonia, Michigan, has four worship services on Sunday morning. Grace Baptist Church located in Simi Valley, California, has six worship services a week in its auditorium that seats 225 worshipers (Wednesday night, Friday night, Saturday night, two Sunday morning services, and Monday night).

Some use the multiservices to conduct different types of worship services. Stephen Hower, Saint John's Lutheran Church, West County, Saint Louis, Missouri, had the traditional Lutheran liturgical services, plus a seeker-sensitive service. Realizing that different expressions of worship attract people of different cultures, age, or class background, the multiservice worship programs will influence worship in the church. It will (1) make the church more tolerant because we reach people according to their background and (2) segregate the church into divisions because we keep people with their own rather than putting them with people of different backgrounds to enrich them.

Multicultural

As more and more cultural groups immigrate to the United States, their presence demands that the church reach and evangelize them. Many churches, specifically urban churches, are having a church service in a different language or targeting various ethnic-linguistic minorities. Churches are adding specific worship services for Hispanics, Koreans, Chinese, Japanese, Laotians, Cambodians, etc. According to C. Peter Wagner, professor at Fuller Theological Seminary, the number of Korean language churches in the United States had grown from two hundred in 1980 to approximately four thousand by 1995. The number of Korean language theological seminaries in the United States has jumped from zero to approximately fifty in fifteen years.

The presence of minorities in America that represent a different culture and different language will force the traditional American churches: (1) to reach out to them, (2) to incorporate them, (3) to involve them in ministry to their own, (4) to adapt to their culture, and (5) to let them change us or we change them. The presence of minorities will change the expression of worship, even the face of worship. Their musical instruments, their dress, and the way they phrase their ideas will influence our worship. Their food, the way they relate to one another, and their customs will influence the way we fellowship with them and incorporate them into the local body of Christ.

Multimedia

America has moved from a print society to an electronic society. Worshipers have evolved from getting most of the data by reading to getting most of their information from television and the computer. The way young people learn about the world and God will influence the way they worship God. Youth are accustomed to learning by experiencing, seeing, touching, feeling, and doing. No longer can we reach them with lineal educational experiences—reading and talking.

Since our youth learn by multiple methods, the church is turning to multimedia in worship. Today's youth learn by watching activities, events, and daily life on television. The church is using drama, skits, characterization, and short plays in worship services. Since they are influenced by music during the week, the church is using contemporary music to attract, teach, involve, and entertain.

Churches will use more video-filmed announcements, testimonies, and even "short subjects" to reinforce the sermon. Churches will continue to use overhead or slide projectors for music and Scripture reading. Some pastors are getting outstanding sermon support from rear-screen projection to enhance communications, including sermon outlines, maps, pictures, landscapes, time lines, and other eye-appealing helps.

Urbanization

Until recently, the American church had been driven by rural values and thinking. The worship service was held at 11:00 A.M. because of the cows—farmers had to get up early to milk; then they fed the stock, did their chores, ate breakfast, and took a bath. This required time, so the appropriate time to begin Sunday school was 9:45 A.M., and the worship followed at 11:00 A.M. Today, most urban churches still hold worship at 11:00 A.M.

As our nation is becoming more urbanized, metropolitan city values are influencing the church. More and more Bible study is being done in cell groups instead of adult Sunday school classes. Rather than sitting in folding chairs, lined up in rows, listening to a Bible lesson, contemporary America prefers the informality of a home TLC (Tender Loving Care) group. Rick Warren, pastor of Saddleback Church, Mission Viejo, California, says, "Put a guy in a tie and coat, sit him in a classroom, and he'll never say a word." But Warren adds, "Put the same guy on a couch in someone's family room, give him a cup of coffee, and he'll talk your arm off."

The dynamics of body life worship will continue to grow because Americans can't build large educational buildings and won't attend structured classes. As our nation continues the trend toward informality, cells will grow in popularity. Body life services will attract more and more with the increase of anonymity, the by-product of urbanization.

Multiexpression

Sunday morning worship will continue to vary from street to street, from ethnic community to ethnic community. One church will remind you of an eighteenth-century European service. Another church across town will have an upbeat church service that is free-wheeling and contemporary.

Some churches will meet in humble frame buildings on dirt streets. Others will meet in soaring cathedrals with spires and stained-glass windows. Some will have a "do-it-yourself" variety of worship with lay preachers and a simple format. Other churches will continue traditional American mainline Protestant forms. Still others will follow the body life model with its emphasis on fellowship.

Religious intensity will continue to vary from apathy in dying churches to the fervency of revivalistic preaching in fundamentalist churches. The not-so-traditional ethnic sect, such as the Mennonite and Amish, will continue its family traditions. The cathedral will demand reverence. Those worshiping in a family living room will emphasize hospitality and friendliness. Charismatic churches will generate excitement, and the "quiet liturgical" churches will demand meditation and reflective worship.

Religious feelings will be as different as the intensity each reflect. Some churches will always feel like a New England Puritan congregation with a few hymns, prayers, followed by a sermon. Other churches will feel like school with people taking notes as the pastor explains the Bible with an overhead projector. Some churches will feel like a self-help therapy session with listeners searching for healing of wounds and reconciliation of relationships. The minister is the counselor with the spiritual gift of mercy-showing. Still other churches will sing the songs of their culture; they will sway and play the tambourine. Some will smile to the strumming of a guitar, or the ultimate, a mariachi band. Still some of the people will shout and chant, with the preacher acting like a cheerleader, guiding the congregation in praises and participatory response.

The differences in churches are deeper than the differences in doctrinal distinctives or the separation between denominations. There are cultural and social differences that affect the way they worship. There is such a vast cultural difference between people that we would only expect they would worship differently.

Each past generation has fought its own theological battle. This means that theological issues that divided the church were carefully examined by the church. Good men examined them carefully, disagreed passionately, and finally exhausted every shade of meaning. Thereafter, the issues may still divide good men, but then they understood the implications that divided them, and they accepted one another and went their separate ways. They stopped fighting over their disagreement. They loved one another in their diversity.

That battle today is over worship.

Final Word

Why is it when leaders get their hands on religion, one of the first things they want to do is to use religion to control people. First, religious leaders want to put people in their place, and second, they want to keep them in their place. Too often the church is guilty of manipulation and coercion to bring people into line. The church uses worship to control people, rather than allowing worship to release people and give them freedom.

Jesus did not come to set up an organization with rules. He is life, and came to give us life, freedom from addiction, and the excitement of having our sins forgiven. Jesus did not come to force people to conform to outward laws. He came with a radically different approach; He offered people escape from selfishness, pettiness, and sin—to live free in Christ. Jesus gives us a new desire to fellowship with God and to worship God. Jesus offers His followers the privilege of touching God in worship and having God touch them.

The New Testament is different from the rule-keeping ways of the Old Testament. Jesus made people want to serve Him rather than demanding outward conformity. The new translation of Scripture called *The Message* translates it,

> I tried keeping rules and working my head off to please God, and it didn't work. So I quit being a "lawman" so that I could be God's man. Christ's life showed me how and enabled me to it. I identified myself completely with him. Indeed, I had been crucified with Christ. My ego is no longer central. It is no longer important that I appear righteous for you or have your good opinion, and I am no longer driven to impress God. Christ lives in me. The

life you see me living is not "mine" but it is lived by faith in the Son of God, who loved me and gave himself for me (Gal. 2:19–20).

Sometimes our young people rebel in church because they don't like our outward services. They mock a hymn they don't understand. Because they read about a minister that has fallen, they have questions about the pastor down the street. Because they don't get anything from the sermon, they call it boring and uninteresting. Because they are angry when the man of God preaches against sin in their lives, they lash out at the church.

Why is it so natural for young people to be rebellious? The baby is born with a clenched fist, and its cry seems to say, "No!" Like a rock on a string that is flung around the head with centrifugal force, youth fly away from God. Yet at the same time, God's compelling love is a centripetal force that pulls people back into harmony with Him. Like water that flows toward the center of a whirlpool, people are pulled into the presence of God.

Young people rebel and are confused as they cast off restraints. Their nature and culture pull them away from God, while inner thoughts and fears drive them to seek Him. The young rebel would like Jesus Christ. He was as antibureaucratic as they come. He condemned the religious sham of His day, as young people condemn today's empty worship sham. Jesus was antiestablishment and antiform. In both His teaching and His life, He cut through man-made form to get back to the simple relationship of God and man. But the problem is that the revolution of Jesus Christ against the dead formalism of His day has forgotten its revolutionary roots. The movement that was to become Christianity has become outwardly a monument.

The church that should be antiestablishment and revolutionary has become what it was originally against. Jesus took His movement out of the buildings (the temple and synagogues) and made it a movement of the streets. Now we have taken it back into buildings and hidden it behind stained-glass barriers. Buildings are not wrong, for there must be protection from the elements and there must be a location for the ecclesia to assemble. But we have made the constructed buildings the central core of who we are and what we do.

Christianity is not its buildings, religious meetings, or forms of worship. Jesus would still tell us, "It's who you are and the way you live that count before God. Your worship must engage your spirit in the pursuit of truth. That's the kind of people the Father is out looking for: these who are simply and honestly themselves before Him in their worship. God is sheer being itself—Spirit. Those who worship Him must do it out of their very being, their spirits, their true selves, in adoration" (John 4:22–24, *The Message*).

Glossary of Terms

administration, gift of. Administration is the management of human, physical, and financial resources through planning, organizing, leading, and controlling. Planning involves projecting the future; establishing objectives; developing policies, programs, procedures, and schedules for accomplishing those objectives; and budgeting adequate resources for the task. Organization involves developing an organizational foundation, delegating responsibilities, and establishing interpersonal relationships. Leading involves making decisions; communicating ideas; and selecting, enlisting, training, and motivating people. Controlling involves establishing performance standards; then measuring, evaluating, and correcting performance on the basis of those standards. Those who are gifted in administration are effective managers.

agent of regeneration. The Holy Spirit is the agent of regeneration—the member of the Trinity most active in the actual regeneration of the believer.

anointing of the Holy Spirit. When a believer yields to God, and in faith asks to be filled with the Holy Spirit (Eph. 5:18–19), God will give power to accomplish a task. The filling of the Spirit is also called the anointing of the Spirit. The anointing is directed as a preparation for a specific task. It is a divine enablement for a specific act of service. The implication of this designation is that of repeated anointings. This is illustrated by David, who was anointed more than once.

Bible expositional church. A unique worship style paradigm for church ministry that emphasizes strong Bible teaching from the pulpit, often accompanied with an expository Bible teaching emphasis in other aspects of the church ministry.

Body Life Church. A unique worship style paradigm for church ministry, emphasizing fellowship relationships between Christians usually nurtured through an extensive cell group ministry at the core of all the church does in ministry.

bridging growth. The increase of the church membership by planting new churches in cultures different from the culture of the base church; represented in two degrees: first degree (designated as E-2 evangelism)—in cultures somewhat different from the base church; second degree (designated as E-3 evangelism)—in cultures greatly different from the base church.

carriers of revival. The phrase *carriers of revival* has been coined to describe the means by which the spirit of revival may be transferred from one place to another. There appear to be at least three types of carriers that may be identified and utilized to create a desire for revival. These include (CR-1) individuals who have themselves experienced revival; (CR-2) authentic accounts of revival experiences; and (CR-3) anointed literature that motivates others to begin working toward revival.

celebration. The gathering of the church collective in its primary function of worship and praise to God; the sum of worshipers represents the whole church family. Also used to describe the quality of contemporary worship in contrast to other worship styles.

cell. The foundational unit of a church's infrastructure, sometimes called a kinship circle. A cell is a small group of eight to twelve believers functioning in a manner that establishes spiritual accountability and provides intimacy in fellowship. Most generic cells have a secondary function, such as Bible study, prayer, training, etc. A technical cell usually meets outside the church building and not on Sunday to carry out its task of ministry.

church. An assembly of professed believers, in whom Christ dwells, under the discipline of the Word of God, organized to carry out the Great Commission, administer the ordinances, and minister with spiritual gifts.

church extension. Church growth through a strategy of planting new churches.

church growth. The discipline that investigates the nature, function, health, and death of Christian churches as they relate specifically to the effective implementation of God's Commission to "make disciples of all the nations" (Matt. 28:19). Church growth is simultaneously a theological conviction and an applied science, striving to combine the eternal principles of God's Word with the best insights of contemporary social and behavioral sciences, employing as its initial frame of reference the foundational work done by Donald McGavran and his colleagues.

church growth: social science. Since about 1975, the Church Growth Movement has grown into public recognition for several reasons. First, superchurches have emerged on the scene and become influential in determining and applying Church Growth strategy. Second, there is a growing interest in the science and practice of church planting. Third, there seems to be more exposure by media to growing churches in general than two decades ago. At the same time the Church Growth Movement has become a discipline, and it has become more sophisticated as it uses both theological and sociological research to examine churches to determine principles of growth.

Church Growth is a behavioral science. As such, it follows the scientific method of inquiry, as do the other natural sciences (e.g., psychology, sociology, etc.). The scientific method involves five steps. First, data must be gathered by the Church Growth researcher. This involves finding all of the facts about one source of church growth, or all the facts about why there is no growth. Second, the data are examined for causes and effects. At this place the researcher determines if when the facts are repeated, they will bring about the same results in growth. If they do, it leads to the third step where the researcher suggests a hypotheses is found. This is a suggested principle or law that causes church growth. (The word *hypotheses* comes from *hypo,* meaning "to propose" and *theses* meaning "an unproven law.") The fourth step is to test the suggested law to see if it is functional, workable, and produces the same results in all situations. When the results are consistent, the fifth step leads to establishing the results as a law or principle that will produce evangelism and church growth or, when the law is broken, will cause a church to plateau or deteriorate.

church growth, types of.

1. Internal—growth of Christians in grace, relationship to God, and to one another.

2. Expansion—growth of the local congregation by the evangelization of non-Christians within its ministry area.

3. Extension—growth of the church by the establishment of daughter churches within the same general homogeneous group.

4. Bridging—growth of the church by establishing churches in different cultural areas.

classifications of revival. The six major classifications of revival based on the apparent causal factors of that revival include (R-1) revivals that may be a response to the discovery, comprehension, and application of a particular doctrine; (R-2) revivals that may be led by a charismatic leader; (R-3) revivals that may be a response to a problematic condition; (R-4) revivals that may be a response to a revived core of believers; (R-5) revivals that may be attributed to interventional prayer; and (R-6) revivals that may be a response to "signs and wonders."

congregational church. A unique worship style paradigm for church ministry that places emphasis on lay people to carry out worship, Christian education, fellowship, and evangelism in its ministry strategy. Often congregational churches are small, single-cell churches because of their de-emphasis on leadership and the high emphasis on lay ministry.

conversion. Participation by non-Christians in a genuine decision for Christ, a sincere turning from the old life and sin, and a determined purpose to live as Christ would have people live.

- Individual Conversion—the evangelization of one person at a time through individual counseling.
- Multi-Individual—many people participate in the act, each individual makes up his or her mind, debates with others, and decides to either accept or reject Christianity.

discipling. Bringing people to a personal relationship with Jesus Christ. A more refined classification follows:

D-1 The turning of a non-Christian society for the first time to Christ.

D-2 The turning of any individual from nonfaith to faith in Christ and his or her incorporation in a church.

D-3 The teaching to existing Christians as much of the truths of the Bible as possible, helping them grow in grace.

evangelism. Communicating the gospel in an understandable manner, and motivating a person to respond to Christ and become a responsible member of His church.

evangelism, gift of. Communicating the gospel in the power of the Holy Spirit to unconverted persons at their point of need with the intent of effecting conversions. These conversions take place as individuals repent of their sin and put their trust in God through Jesus Christ, to accept Him as their Savior. Normally, those who are converted determine to serve the Lord in the fellowship of a local church. Those who are gifted in evangelism are effective in making disciples of various types of people through their personal evangelistic efforts.

evangelistic church. A unique worship style paradigm for church ministry that views evangelism as its primary reason for being and seeks to accomplish the Great Commission through unique outreach efforts to specific target groups in its community.

exhortation, gift of. Exhortation is urging others to act on the basis of their faith in God, advising others how to accomplish specific goals in life and/or ministry, cautioning others against actions that are potentially dangerous, and motivating others in the Christian life and ministry. Those gifted in exhortation usually develop simple strategies to accomplish goals and effectively encourage and motivate others to remain faithful in their service for God.

gift assimilation. Many Christians will be saved in a church or will begin attending a church where the dominant spiritual gift in the church is different from the Christian's dominant spiritual gift. Then because of example, influence, teaching, and other factors, the Christian begins to assimilate a spiritual gift that was not indigenous or dominant to him or her.

gift colonization. Because of information about types of worship styles that is available and the accessibility of that church worship style because of improved transportation, believers tend to gravitate to a worship style that reflects their dominant spiritual gift; hence, the church becomes a colony of like-gifted believers.

gift gravitation. In the American culture that is dominated by information (the Internet) and transportation (the interstate), people began attending a local church where the dominant spiritual gift that is exercised in the congregation is their dominant spiritual gift.

giving, gift of. Giving is investing financial and other resources in ways that further the purposes of God through individuals and/or ministries. Givers are inclined to be generous in financially underwriting a wide variety of ministry projects.

homogeneous units/groups. A group of people with a similar social trademark, which necessarily bonds them together as a whole.

instrument of regeneration. The Scriptures are the instrument of regeneration—the tool used by the Holy Spirit to produce new life in the believer.

liturgical church. A unique worship style paradigm for church ministry that seeks to draw from a rich tradition of historic expressions of worship including ancient hymns, creeds, and prayers. Liturgy comes from *latreuo,* which means "to serve or minister." In a liturgical church God is the center of worship and worshipers minister to Him, not primarily themselves. Liturgical churches are most often found among the Catholic and mainline Protestant denominations.

people movement. Results from the joint decision of a number of individuals from the same people group, which enables them to become Christian without social dislocation, while remaining in full contact with their non-Christian relatives, thus enabling other segments of that people group, across the years, to come to similar decisions and form Christian churches made up primarily of members of that people group.

prophecy, gift of. Prophecy is communicating and applying biblical truth to a specific situation or circumstance. An individual "speaks edification and exhortation and comfort to men" (1 Cor. 14:3) through exercising this gift. Also, this area of giftedness appears to involve some measure of the enabling gift of faith (Rom. 12:6). Those gifted in this area are usually able to discern problems and apply appropriate biblical principles to help alleviate the problems.

receptive people. Those who are positive toward the gospel message as a result of social dislocation, personal crisis, or internal working of the Holy Spirit. They are open to hearing and obeying the gospel of Jesus Christ.

redemption and lift. A phenomenon that occurs when a person or group becomes a Christian and thereby is lifted out of his or her former environment and separated from it in social and economic respects.

This causes a gap between the new Christian and his or her unsaved friends.

renewal church. A unique worship style paradigm for church ministry usually characterized by informality in worship and the wide use of contemporary praise choruses in its worship services with a view of reviving the worshiper. The Renewal Church believes worship is a two-way street. When God is worshiped, His presence will enter the worship service; and in the presence of God, the needs of the worshiper are met.

revival. An evangelical revival is an extraordinary work of God in which Christians tend to repent of their sins as they become intensely aware of His presence in their midst. They manifest a positive response to God in renewed obedience to the known will of God, resulting in both a deepening of their individual and corporate experience with God and an increased concern for the spiritual welfare of themselves and others within their community. The popular description of revival is "God pouring out Himself on His people." Revival is an experience that is taught in Scripture and has a historical precedent in the Christian church. It is a state of spiritual enthusiasm or excitement for Christ. Yet the experience of revival is not a continuing experience. The normal church, no matter how spiritual, tends to need a revival of interest, a revival of soul-winning, or a revival of believers. Revival is a return to one's original Christian experience, or a return to original Christianity as found in the Book of Acts.

serving, gift of. Serving is discerning and meeting the spiritual and physical needs of individuals. Those gifted in this ministry are supportive of others and concerned with helping them in any way possible. They usually enjoy manual tasks.

shepherding, gift of. Shepherding is compassionately caring for others in your sphere of influence by providing spiritual guidance, nourishment, and protection from potentially destructive individuals or influences. Those who have this gift readily express their concern for others and are often looked to for spiritual counsel and guidance.

showing mercy, gift of. Showing mercy is discovering emotionally stressed and distressed individuals and ministering to their emotional needs. Mercy-showers express sympathy, empathy, and spiritual ministry to help alleviate the inner pain that is causing a person's dysfunctional emotional response. Those gifted in showing mercy tend to be drawn toward hurting people and are somewhat effective in helping others rebuild their lives.

spiritual gifts. When Paul addressed the Corinthians on the subject, he used five different Greek words to describe the nature of spiritual gifts (1 Cor. 12:1–7): (1) *pneumatikon,* which is translated "spiritual" (1 Cor. 12:1), describes the character of these gifts as spiritual; (2) *charismata,* which is translated "gifts" (1 Cor. 12:4), emphasizes gifts as God's free and gracious gifts; (3) *diakonia,* translated "ministries" (1 Cor. 12:5), reveals gifts as opportunities for ministry; (4) *energema,* translated "activities" (1 Cor. 12:6), suggests that gifts are an endowment of God's power or energy; (5) *phanerosis,* translated "manifestation" (1 Cor. 12:7), means that gifts are evidence of God working through us.

When the various biblical lists of spiritual gifts are examined, there appear to be three kinds of spiritual gifts. First are the miraculous gifts, such as tongues and healing. Second, there are four enabling gifts that each Christian appears to have to some degree (discernment, faith, knowledge, and wisdom). These gifts enhance the third group of spiritual gifts, the task-oriented gifts. Task-oriented gifts are our tools for effectiveness as part of the ministry team and include evangelism, prophecy, teaching, exhortation, shepherding, showing mercy, serving, giving, and administration.

superchurch. Churches that have demonstrated a strong desire and ability to grow, that have many agencies for growth (synergistic approach to evangelism), that are located on a large church campus, and that have a varied staff of professionals. Superchurches usually number in the thousands.

teaching, gift of. Teaching is communication of biblical principles in the power of the Holy Spirit to others and demonstration of the relevance of those principles to the specific needs represented. Those gifted in the area of teaching tend to be diligent students of the Scriptures and to have accumulated a thorough understanding of biblical principles as a result of their consistent study habits.

winnable people. Those who are considered receptive to the gospel; those who will respond.

worship. Worship is a face-to-face encounter with the living God based on a regeneration experience, prompted by the Holy Spirit, and resulting in the exhaltation of God's glory. Simply speaking, worship is giving the worthship to God that He deserves because He is God. Therefore, worship should be an emotional, intellectual, and volitional response to God.

Because of the relationship between worshiper and God who is worshiped, worship is a growing thing and a dynamic entity. Worship is personal, and true worship cannot be divorced from the worshiper. Worship, we might say, is an earnest effort to re-create the conditions and experiences that have been found to deepen a person's relationship with God.

Worship involves the intellectual process, but it is more than mere knowledge of God. Worship stirs the emotions, but is more than the expression of passion. Worship comes from a person's choice to surrender his or her will to God, but is more than a mere decision. The heart is moved by biblical facts to re-create the fundamental human experiences of praise, adoration, and exhaltation of God for who He is and what He has done for humans in general and the worshiper in specific.

Biblical Words for Worship

An important step in developing a biblical theology of worship is examination of the biblical words used to describe worship in Scripture. Many of these Hebrew and Greek words emphasize various dimensions of the worship experience. Only as these terms are understood can we more fully understand the concept of worship. The Old Testament uses four Hebrew words and the New Testament uses four Greek terms to describe worship.

Worship in the Old Testament

The Old Testament uses four Hebrew terms and one Aramaic word translated "worship." The root idea of these terms is that of a reverential attitude of the worshiper, often expressed physically by the act of bowing or prostrating one's self before a superior. Also implied in these terms is the idea of adoration, obedience, and service.

1. *Shachad.* The Hebrew word *shachad* literally means "depress," "bow down," or "prostrate." It is used ninety-five times in the Old Testament to describe people in worship (Exod. 4:31). The root idea of this term for worship is that of humbling one's self before God or someone else.

2. *Tsaghadh.* The Hebrew word *tsaghadh* and Aramaic term *tseghidh* are based on the idea of falling down and prostrating one's self (Isa. 44:15, 17, 19; Dan. 3:5–7, 10, 15). Also implied in the meaning of these terms is the idea of humble service.

3. *ʿAbhadh.* The Hebrew word *ʿabhadh* is based on a root describing work, labor, or service. It is used in the Old Testament to describe both pagan worship (2 Kings 10; 19:21ff.) and the worship of God (Isa. 19:21, 23).

4. *ʿAcabh.* The Hebrew word *ʿacabh* is translated "worship" once in the Old Testament (Jer. 44:19). This word means to carve, fabricate, or fashion

and is used to describe the making of idols. In the context of the Old Testament, this is a clearly inferior expression of worship and not part of the legitimate worship of God.

Worship in the New Testament

In the New Testament, there are four principle Greek terms used to describe various aspects of the worship experience.

1. *Proskuneo.* The Greek word *proskuneo* is a compound composed of *pros,* meaning "toward," and *kuneo,* meaning "to kiss." The word means "to make obeisance" or "do reverence to" and is most often simply translated "worship" in the New Testament. J. N. Darby used the expression "do homage" when translating this term in his English translation of the Bible.

The Use of *Proskuneo* in the New Testament

Reverence to God: Matt. 4:10; John 4:21–24; 1 Cor. 14:25; Rev. 4:10; 5:14; 7:11; 11:16; 19:10; 22:9

Reverence to Christ: Matt. 2:2, 8, 11; 8:2; 9:18; 14:33; 15:25; 20:20; 28:9, 17; John 9:38; Heb. 1:6

Reverence to a Man: Matt. 18:26

Reverence to the Dragon: Rev. 13:4

Reverence to the Beast: Rev. 13:4, 8, 12, 15; 14:9, 11; 16:2

Reverence to Demons: Rev. 9:20

Reverence to Idols: Acts 7:43

2. *Sebomai/Sembazomai.* The words *sembomai* and *sembazomai* are related terms and convey the idea of revering with an emphasis on a feeling of awe or devotion often associated with worship. This sense of awe or devotion is so strongly implied in these words that four times in the New Testament the word *sebomai* is translated "devout" (Acts 13:43, 50; 17:4, 17).

The Use of *Sebomai* in the New Testament

Devotion to God: Matt. 15:9; Mark 7:7; Acts 16:14; 18:7, 13

Devotion to a Goddess: Acts 19:27

The Use of *Sembazomai* in the New Testament

Devotion to a Creature: Rom. 1:25

3. *Latreuo.* The word *latreuo* means to "serve" or "render religious service or homage." Although this word is often translated "worship" in the New Testament, it is most often translated "serve" and is related to *latris,*

which means "a hired servant." This word tends to emphasize worship as a service to God on the part of the worshiper.

The Use of *Latreuo* in the New Testament

Serving God: Matt. 4:10; Luke 1:74; 2:37; 4:8; Acts 7:7; 24:14; 26:7; 27:23; Rom. 1:9; Phil. 3:3; 2 Tim. 1:3; Heb. 9:14; 12:28; Rev. 7:15; 22:3

Serving the Stars: Acts 7:42

Serving the Creature: Rom. 1:25

Serving the Law: Heb. 8:5; 9:9; 10:2; 13:10

4. *Eusebeo.* The fourth verb used in the New Testament to describe worship is *eusebeo,* meaning "to act piously toward." The apostle Paul claimed the Athenians worshiped the "Unknown God" in this way when addressing them on Mars Hill (Acts 17:23). The same Greek word is also used by Paul to identify the obligation of children and grandchildren toward their widowed mother or grandmother (1 Tim. 5:4). The root idea of this word in both places where it is used seems to be that of showing honor toward one who should be honored.

The Use of *Eusebeo* in the New Testament

Pious in Faith: Acts 17:23

Pious in Family: 1 Tim. 5:4

Christian Leaders on Worship

Wonder is the basis of worship.

Thomas Carlyle

There is a use for ritual in a man's religious life. When a man is in a right relationship to God, ritual is an assistance; the place of worship and the atmosphere are both conducive to worship.

Oswald Chambers

Reverence towards God makes men natural and simple to each other. There is a modest yet unabashed naturalness of manner which occasionally distinguishes spiritual persons, into whatever company they are come. A man will hardly ever be awkward in public, who in secret pays habitual reverent court to God. Habitual reverence is the high breeding of the spiritual life.

F. W. Faber

It is commonly assumed that, provided only we repair to our church or chapel, the performance of the work of adoration is a thing that may be taken for granted. But the work of Divine Worship, so far from being a thing of course even among those who outwardly address themselves to its performance, is one of the most arduous which the human spirit can possibly set about.

William E. Gladstone

Worship is an opportunity for man to invite God's power and presence to move among those worshiping Him.

Jack W. Hayford

Take heed, then, often to come together to give thanks to God, and show forth His praise. For when ye come frequently together in the same place, the powers of Satan are destroyed, and his "fiery darts" urging to sin fall back ineffectual. For your concord and harmonious faith prove his destruction, and the torment of his assistants.

Ignatius of Antioch

All Christian worship, public and private, should be an intelligent response to God's self-revelation in his words and works recorded in Scripture.

D. Martyn Lloyd-Jones

May all who use these hymns experience, at all times, the blessed effects of complying with the Apostle Paul's injunction (Eph. 5:18–19), "Be filled with the Spirit, speaking to yourselves in psalms, and hymns, and spiritual songs, singing and making melody in your heart to the Lord." Yea, may they anticipate, while here below, though in a humble and imperfect strain, the song of the blessed above, who, being redeemed out of every kindred, and tongue, and people, and nation, and having washed their robes, and made them white in the blood of the Lamb, are standing before the throne, and singing in perfect harmony with the many angels about it (Rev. 5:9–12 and 7:9--14), "Worthy is the Lamb that was slain, to receive power, and riches, and wisdom, and strength, and honor, and glory, and blessing, for ever and ever. Amen!"

Moravian Hymnal (1789)

The true ideal of worship is that of man communing with God.

G. Campbell Morgan

Again, it is not a thing which man can decide, whether he will be a worshiper or not. A worshiper he must be; the only question is what will he worship? Every man worships—is born a worshiper.

Frederick W. Robertson

The best public worship is that which produces the best private Christianity.

J. C. Ryle

In the act of worship, God communicates His presence to His people.

J. Oswald Sanders

We evangelicals do not know much about worship. Evangelism is our specialty, not worship. We have little sense of the greatness of Almighty God. We tend to be cocky, flippant, and proud. And our worship services are often ill-prepared, slovenly, mechanical, perfunctory, and dull. . . . Much of our public worship is ritual without reality, form without power, religion without God.

John R. W. Stott

To worship is to quicken the conscience by the holiness of God, to feed the mind with the truth of God, to purge the imagination by the beauty of God, to open the heart to the love of God, to devote the will to the purpose of God. All this is gathered up in that emotion which cleanses us from selfishness because it is the most self-less of all emotions—adoration.

William Temple

Worship is the exercise of the mind in the contemplation of God in which wonder and awe play an important part in stretching and enlarging our vision, or in opening up our conceptual forms to take in that which by its nature far outruns them.

T. F. Torrance

What is worship? Worship is to feel in your heart and express in some appropriate manner a humbling but delightful sense of admiring awe and astonished wonder and overpowering love in the presence of that most ancient Mystery, that Majesty which philosophers call the First Cause, but which we call Our Father Which Art in Heaven.

A. W. Tozer

The worship of God is nowhere defined in Scripture. . . . it is not confined to praise; broadly it may be regarded as the direct acknowledgment of God, of His nature, attributes, ways and claims, whether by the outgoing of the heart in praise and thanksgiving or by deed done in such acknowledgment.

W. E. Vine

The worship of God is not a rule of safety—it is an adventure of the spirit, a flight after the unattainable.

Alfred North Whitehead

Worship is the believer's response of all that he is—mind, emotions, will, and body—to all that God is and says and does. This response has its mystical side in subjective experience, and its practical side in objective obedience to God's revealed truth. It is a loving response that is balanced by the fear of the Lord, and it is a deepening response as the believer comes to know God better.

Warren W. Wiersbe

Study Guide

by Douglas Porter

Worship Wars is a study of the tensions in the evangelical church today over the way we worship God. The author, Elmer L. Towns, presents it as "a descriptive book that reflects the trends and tensions in our contemporary church over worship practice." He wrote the book to help the reader "return to your worship style and do it better."

This study guide has been prepared to help a church leadership team or worship team work through the various issues raised in its own church. Each session is based on one of the twelve chapters. Each group member should have a personal copy of the book and read through the chapter before the study session. The pastor or worship leader can use the questions and worship projects to guide group members through a better understanding of the chapter contents and how the principles of worship raised in each chapter can be applied to enhance their church's worship.

Session One

Study Questions

The first chapter surveys the six new worship paradigms being used by evangelical churches in America today. Understanding how and why others worship God the way they do will help us fit our own worship style into context and make us more tolerant of others who choose to worship God differently.

1. Towns writes, "Culture is influencing the Church more than the Church is influencing the culture." How does that make you feel? What aspects of our culture have begun to have an impact on your church?

2. This chapter describes six worship styles. Which of these comes closest to describing the dominant worship style in your church?

3. Towns writes, "People with a dominant spiritual gift choose a church where their personal dominant gift is also the dominant corporate gift. That's why they feel comfortable in a particular style of worship." What are the dominant spiritual gifts operating in your church?

4. If your work required you to relocate to another state, what would you look for in selecting a new church home? If there are several things on your list, try to prioritize them in order of importance. Which items listed are essential? Which items listed are your preferences that you might be willing to overlook?

5. What is there about your church that attracts people to your worship services? Are there aspects of your typical worship service that hinder people in their worship of God? At what point in your worship service do people feel closest to God?

Worship Project

The successful church of the future will be the church that does what it does best most often. As you review the data collected in your discussion, make a list of those things your church does best when it worships God. Then make a list of the aspects of your worship service that hinder people in their worship of God.

In many cases, that which your church does best may be the mission God is calling your church to fulfill in your community. If you have not already done so, take time to write a draft mission statement for your church that briefly describes the primary function of your church and the means by which you are most likely to accomplish that goal. As you work through this study, you may wish to edit that statement as you gain new insights into worship.

Read your draft mission statement before planning this week's worship service. After you have outlined the service, read the statement again. How does that worship service reflect the mission of your church? Are there aspects of the service that detract from the mission? If you find this project challenging, take heart. Most of us need to run through this exercise for several months before it begins to come more naturally.

Session Two

In chapter 2, Towns discusses his own personal pilgrimage of worship. Most of us who have been Christians for long have experienced similar changes in our relationship with God. In this session, we will focus on our individual worship experiences to identify the worship style that best meets our present needs.

Study Questions

1. Towns begins this chapter describing his own worship experience in a variety of different church types. Which of these churches appealed to you most as you read the chapter? What was it about those churches that you found most attractive?

2. Some of the churches described probably appeal to you very much; others, not at all. Which of the churches described would you be most unlikely to attend? What is there about that church that hindered your experience of worship?

3. Towns asks his students three questions when he teaches on worship styles. Let's use those questions to understand our own pilgrimage of worship. First, think back to the church that was influential in your conversion. How would you describe that church? Which worship type was dominant in its worship service?

4. The second question directs us to examine our present worship experience. How would you describe the dominant worship style of your church?

5. From time to time, most of us find ourselves in transition in our Christian life. Let's adapt the third question slightly to help us identify where we are moving in worship. Which worship style would you prefer to become dominant as your church grows in its worship experience?

Worship Project

The title page to chapter 2 reminds us, "It is not *how* you worship, it is *who* you worship." Let's remember to keep our focus as we look at the changing worship styles in our church. Does your worship team agree on the way your church would feel most comfortable worshiping God? If not, how could you achieve such a consensus? How close is your church to that preferred worship style?

If you try to make major changes in your worship style without preparing your people, conflict will break out at some level in your church. Your goal is to avoid a worship war and focus on worshiping God. If you decide to make changes, be careful to prepare your people for change. Later in this study series, we will look at specific ways to tap into the strengths of various worship styles.

Session Three

In chapter 3, Towns discusses some of the research that has shaped his conclusions about differing worship styles practiced by American Christians. In this session, we will focus on this research in order to learn more about the character of the church in which we worship.

Study Questions

1. Towns writes, "We worship differently because of cultural differences." What are the dominant ethnic-linguistic people groups in your church? How do their cultural backgrounds influence the way they tend to worship God?

2. Spiritual gifting is a second factor that influences our worship style. What are the dominant spiritual gifts in your church? How does that gift colony influence the worship style of your church?

3. Before leaving the area of gifts, let's get a little more personal. What is/are your dominant spiritual gift(s)? How do they compare with the dominant gift expressions in the church? If given the freedom to do so, how would you worship God differently? Would these modifications help or hinder others as they worship God?

4. Our understanding of the Scriptures also colors the way we worship God. How do the distinctives of your church or denomination influence the way you worship God?

5. Within many churches, a dominant majority and more docile minorities worship together. Consider those who are not part of the dominant ethnic-linguistic culture or gift colony in your church or those who come to your church from different faith backgrounds. What barriers must they overcome to worship God in your church? How could your church be more accommodating to help them worship God in spirit and in truth?

Worship Project

The worship of God will be cosmopolitan, including people from every nation, tribe, people, and language (Rev. 7:9). To help your people appreciate the contributions of other cultures to the worship of God, plan a worship service that grows out of a different culture, perhaps as part of a missions emphasis. Choose hymns that reflect the values and music styles that would be typically emphasized in that culture. If you have missionaries serving in that part of the world, you may want to have them share a testimony or have focused prayer for that mission field.

After the service, evaluate how well your congregation received this experiment. Did it help them identify better with their missionary or the mission work on that field? Are there aspects of that worship service that should be incorporated into your church worship style? Would it be helpful to your people to repeat this experiment every three or four months to help them gain a deeper appreciation of other cultures or the needs in various mission fields?

Session Four

In chapter 4, Towns walks right into the heart of our worship wars. We must look at tensions that exist or may develop in our church over worship and develop a strategy to bring peace into our worship wars.

Study Questions

1. Towns begins this chapter with several case studies of conflicts over changing worship styles in various churches. Do any of these conflicts sound similar to something your church has experienced? Do any of these conflicts sound like something that could happen in your church?

2. Even in the healthiest of churches, a minority disapproves of what is happening in the church. How are these people expressing their dissatisfaction in your church? What is the basis of their disagreement? Are their concerns legitimate? What can or should your church do to address these concerns?

3. Towns differentiates between theology, principles, and methods. How are these three areas related? How do they differ from each other? How would you distinguish between your theology, principles, and worship methods?

4. Towns concludes this chapter by identifying six specific tensions in worship today. Which applies to your worship style? Do you understand why others are concerned about that issue? How would you respond to that criticism? How do you need to change your worship style in light of what you are learning in this study?

5. Perhaps there have been concerns raised in your church that are not covered in this chapter. Have you taken time to address these concerns? What can and should be done to strengthen the unity within your church to make your church more effective in ministry?

Worship Project

A wise pastor once observed, "If there is conflict in the church, it probably has something to do with the youth or music ministry." It is unfortunate that so many wars have been fought over something as basic as the worship of God. As we apply this chapter to our church, let's look at how we can do a better job managing conflict in this area. Use the questions suggested by Towns on the last page of this chapter as a guide to understanding your worship war and the response you should have to others.

1. Is this a question of *how* we worship or *who* we worship?

2. Is this a question of *preference* or *principle?*

3. Is this a question of cultural *expression* or Christian *essence?*

Session Five

In chapter 5, Towns discusses the Evangelistic Church. This is one of the six ways people choose to "worship the Father in spirit and in truth" today (John 4:23). It may be the way your church chooses to worship God. The purpose of this study session is to understand this worship paradigm. Even if your worship style differs from that of the Evangelistic Church, there are strengths in this paradigm you may wish to incorporate into the style of your church.

Study Questions

1. What is the mission of the Evangelistic Church? How does its worship service reflect this emphasis? How valid is this mission in light of the Scriptures?

2. Every church has its own expectations in worship. What do people expect when they come together to worship in an evangelistic service?

What is the role of the pastor in achieving these expectations? What is the role of the congregation in achieving these expectations?

3. Which spiritual gifts tend to be most dominant in the Evangelistic Church? How would you describe these gifts? How dominant are these gifts in your church?

4. Towns identifies several national church leaders who pastor evangelistic churches. Which churches in your community would you describe as evangelistic? Would your church be included on that list?

5. Each worship style has strengths and weaknesses. What is the dominant strength of the Evangelistic Church? What is its major weakness?

Worship Project

As we look at each of the six worship paradigms, let's use our study time to learn how to tap into the strengths of each worship style. How can your church learn from the Evangelistic Church to become more effective in reaching people for Christ in your community? How would your church respond to a Friend Day—a day set aside to invite unsaved friends to church with them to hear a clear presentation of the gospel? Set a date this fall or spring for a Friend Day in your church and begin making plans for this significant outreach event.

Becoming more evangelistic in your church begins with the leadership becoming more evangelistic. Make a list of the friends, relatives, associates, and neighbors who, to the best of your knowledge, do not know Christ as Savior. Begin praying for these individuals, asking God to give you the opportunity to share the gospel with them. You may be surprised at how God chooses to answer your prayer.

As evangelism becomes a more significant part of your Christian life and witness, begin equipping your people to reach their friends, relatives, associates, and neighbors. You will want to do this about two months before Friend Day to help your people identify those they will bring with them.

If you would describe your church as an evangelistic church, take a closer look at the major weaknesses of this worship paradigm. How effective is your church in discipling those who are reached for Christ through its ministry? What needs to be done to make your church more effective in discipleship training? Make a list of those who could help solve this problem by discipling individuals or a group of new converts. If your church does not already have a plan for discipling new converts that includes a specific curriculum, contact your local curriculum supplier to learn what is available. Also, if those who will be involved in discipling new converts need additional training to equip them for this ministry, be sure to provide the training needed.

Session Six

In chapter 6, Towns discusses the Bible Expositional Church—one of the six paradigms of worship. It may be the way your church chooses to worship God. Even if your worship style differs from that of the Bible Expositional Church, there are strengths in this paradigm you may wish to incorporate into the style of your church.

Study Questions

1. What is the mission of the Bible Expositional Church? How does its worship service reflect this emphasis? How valid is this mission in light of the Scriptures?

2. What do people expect when they come together to worship in a Bible expositional service? What is the role of the pastor in achieving these expectations? What is the role of the congregation in achieving these expectations?

3. Which spiritual gifts tend to be most dominant in the Bible Expositional Church? How would you describe these gifts? How dominant are these gifts in your church?

4. Towns identifies several national church leaders who pastor Bible expositional churches. Which churches in your community would you describe as Bible expositional? Would your church be included on that list?

5. Each worship style has significant strengths and weaknesses. What is the dominant strength of the Bible Expositional Church? What is its major weakness?

Worship Project

As we look at each of the six worship paradigms, let's use our study time to learn how to tap into the strengths of each worship style. How can your church learn from the Bible Expositional Church to become more effective in the systematic teaching of the Scriptures? What structures are in place to make a continued, balanced Bible teaching ministry available to your people? Perhaps this would be a good time to review your Sunday school or cell group curriculum to ensure long-term involvement in these ministries will result in a good understanding of the contents of the Scriptures and a basic understanding of Christian doctrine.

To encourage personal Bible study and teach your people the Scriptures, consider preaching a short series through one of the smaller books of the Bible, the life of a Bible character, or an extended passage of Scripture. Ruth, Jonah, Philippians, and 2 Timothy all lend themselves well to a month of chapter sermons. This discipline will help those not trained in expository preaching begin developing skills in this approach to ministry without making a lifelong commitment to preaching through the Bible. Even if you choose not to be an expository preacher, this project may be worth repeating on an annual basis to encourage your congregation in their own personal Bible study.

If you would describe your church as a Bible expositional church, take a closer look at the major weaknesses of this worship paradigm. How effective is your church in reaching people for Christ and helping them experience the abundance Jesus promised in the Christian life (John 10:10)? Perhaps you need to review session five to look for ways to become more effective in reaching people for Christ. As you plan this week's worship service, choose hymns that help people express their faith at the experience level of their lives. Also, consider challenging your people with a specific project that would stretch them to apply what they are learning to their Christian life (e.g., a Bible reading month or week of prayer).

Session Seven

In chapter 7, Towns discusses another paradigm: the Renewal Church. It may be the way your church chooses to worship God. Even if your worship style differs from that of the Renewal Church, there are strengths in this paradigm you may wish to incorporate into the style of your church.

Study Questions

1. What is the mission of the Renewal Church? How does its worship service reflect this emphasis? How valid is this mission in light of the Scriptures?

2. Every church has its own expectations in worship. What do people expect when they come together to worship in a renewal service? What is the role of the pastor in achieving these expectations? What is the role of the congregation in achieving these expectations?

3. Which spiritual gifts are dominant in the Renewal Church? How would you describe these gifts? How dominant are these gifts in your church?

4. Towns identifies several national church leaders who pastor renewal churches. Which churches in your community would you describe as renewal? Would your church be included on that list?

5. Each worship style has significant strengths and weaknesses. What is the dominant strength of the Renewal Church? What is its major weakness?

Worship Project

As we look at each of the six worship paradigms, let's use our study time to learn how to tap into the strengths of each worship style. How can your church learn from the Renewal Church to help people worship God in a more contemporary way? Does the music style used Sunday morning in your church reflect the musical tastes of your church members during the week? Many more traditional churches have found the quality of their worship services has been enhanced by introducing more contemporary music into a blended worship service, which is a service including both traditional hymns and contemporary choruses.

Follow the guidelines in this chapter in planning your worship service for this Sunday. Don't try to change too much too quickly. If your church does not regularly use praise or Scripture choruses in worship services, carefully choose one chorus to introduce and teach to your congregation. Choose a chorus that fits well with the theme of the message and the tempo of other hymns used in the service. Teach the chorus earlier in the service and use the chorus as a congregational response to the message at the end of the service.

If you would describe your church as a renewal church, take a closer look at the major weaknesses of this worship paradigm. Is your church doctrinally stable? Would the worship project in session 6 help bring doctrinal stability to your congregation?

Session Eight

In chapter 8, Towns discusses the Body Life Church. This is one of the six ways people choose to "worship the Father in spirit and in truth" today (John 4:23). It may be the way your church chooses to worship God. The purpose of this study session is to understand this worship paradigm. Even if your worship style differs from that of the Body Life Church, there are strengths in this paradigm you may wish to incorporate into the style of your church.

Study Questions

1. What is the mission of the Body Life Church? How does its worship service reflect this emphasis? How valid is this mission in light of the Scriptures?

2. Every church has its own expectations in worship. What do people expect when they come together to worship in a body life service? What is the role of the pastor in achieving these expectations? What is the role of the congregation in achieving these expectations?

3. Which spiritual gifts tend to be most dominant in the Body Life Church? How would you describe these gifts? How dominant are these gifts in your church?

4. Towns identifies several national church leaders who pastor Body Life Churches. Which churches in your community would you describe as body life? Would your church be included on that list?

5. Each worship style has significant strengths and weaknesses. What is the dominant strength of the Body Life Church? What is its major weakness?

Worship Project

As we look at each of the six worship paradigms, let's use our study time to learn how to tap into the strengths of each worship style. How can your church learn from the Body Life Church to enhance the quality of fellowship among church members? What are the cell structures within your church infrastructure? Are these groups gathering on a regular basis socially to encourage relationships within the group?

Most noncell churches have existing cells within the congregation even though they have not been so identified. Perhaps they are Sunday school classes or home Bible study groups in your church. To encourage the development of fellowship and involvement in each other's lives within your church, encourage your group leaders to study the "one another" statements of the New Testament to help group members understand their responsibilities to each other.

If you would describe your church as a Body Life Church, take a closer look at the major weaknesses of this worship paradigm. Are areas of your church's life and ministry suffering because of an exclusive commitment to the cell model? Would your families be better served if noncell-type children's and youth ministries were allowed to develop? There are a number of denominational agencies and parachurch ministries that are willing to work with churches in the development of club-type programs that may help you overcome the inherent weakness associated with the cell approach to ministry.

Session Nine

In chapter 9, Towns discusses the Liturgical Church—one of the six paradigms. It may be the way your church chooses to worship God. The purpose of this study session is to understand this worship paradigm. Even if your worship style differs from that of the Liturgical Church, there are strengths in this paradigm you may wish to incorporate into the style of your church.

Study Questions

1. What is the mission of the Liturgical Church? How does its worship service reflect this emphasis? How valid is this mission in light of the Scriptures?

2. Every church has its own expectations in worship. What do people expect when they come together to worship in a liturgical service? What is the role of the pastor in achieving these expectations? What is the role of the congregation in achieving these expectations?

3. Which spiritual gifts tend to be most dominant in the Liturgical Church? How would you describe these gifts? How dominant are these gifts in your church?

4. Towns identifies several national church leaders who pastor liturgical churches. Which churches in your community would you describe as liturgical? Would your church be included on that list?

5. Each worship style has significant strengths and weaknesses. What is the dominant strength of the Liturgical Church? What is its major weakness?

Worship Project

As we look at each of the six worship paradigms, let's use our study time to learn how to tap into the strengths of each worship style. How can your church learn from the Liturgical Church to capitalize on our rich heritage of worship? Survey your worship services for the last two months. When were the hymns used in these services written? Could most be assigned to a period of fifty to one hundred years? What periods of church history are being neglected in your worship service?

Many liturgical churches make use of creedal statements or biblical prayers as part of their worship service. Consider incorporating these expressions of worship into your worship service. You may want to encourage the congregation to recite the Lord's Prayer together as part of the worship service for several weeks as you preach on principles of prayer found in that model prayer. Some pastors have found it helpful to use a biblical blessing to conclude the worship service. Others have taught their congregations the Apostles' Creed as part of a doctrinal series of messages.

If you would describe your church as a liturgical church, take a closer look at the major weaknesses of this worship paradigm. How effective is your church in communicating the gospel to your community? How committed is your church to the Scriptures as the final authority in matters of faith and practice? You may want to review session 5 and 6 to look for ways to become more evangelistic and have a biblical orientation in your ministry.

Session Ten

In chapter 10, Towns discusses the Congregational Church—the last of the six ways people choose to "worship the Father in spirit and in truth" today (John 4:23). It may be the way your church chooses to worship God. The purpose of this study session is to understand this worship paradigm. Even if your worship style differs from that of the Congregational Church, there are strengths in this paradigm you may wish to incorporate into the style of your church.

Study Questions

1. What is the mission of the Congregational Church? How does its worship service reflect this emphasis? How valid is this mission in light of the Scriptures?

2. Every church has its own expectations in worship. What do people expect when they come together to worship in a congregational service? What is the role of the pastor in achieving these expectations? What is the role of the congregation in achieving these expectations?

3. How does a blending of spiritual gifts tend to serve as a bonding agent in the Congregational Church? Does such a blending of gifts exist in your church?

4. Which churches in your community would you describe as congregational? Would your church be included on that list?

5. Each worship style has significant strengths and weaknesses. What is the dominant strength of the Congregational Church? What is its major weakness?

Worship Project

As we look at each of the six worship paradigms, let's use our study time to learn how to tap into the strengths of each worship style. How can your church learn from the Congregational Church to secure greater lay involvement in ministry? What percentage of your present church membership is currently involved in a significant ministry within the church? Are you satisfied with this situation? What percentage would you like to see involved in ministry?

Towns describes a gift-based strategy for enlistment in this chapter. Do you think this strategy could be effective in your church? If your people do not know what their spiritual gifts are, take several weeks to teach your congregation about spiritual gifts. You may want to make use of a Spiritual Gift Inventory Questionnaire to help people identify their gifts. Then consider ministry opportunities available in your church that could be filled by people gifted in specific areas. Using this approach normally results in a deeper and longer lasting commitment to the ministry on the part of those involved.

If you would describe your church as a congregational church, take time to evaluate how well you are doing in achieving a balanced ministry. From time to time, churches will tend to emphasize one aspect of ministry over others. Which part of the ministry is currently being emphasized in your church? Is some area beginning to suffer neglect? Maintaining a balance in ministry is a constant struggle, even in the Congregational Church.

Session Eleven

In chapter 11, Towns explains nineteen important principles that may help us appreciate the way we worship God. Understanding and consistently applying the principles could help us minimize conflict in our churches. The purpose of this session is to help us become more tolerant of others who differ with us on nonessentials.

Study Questions

1. Towns begins this chapter describing four kinds of "worship eyes." As you review his description of each set of eyes, which eyes best describe your attitude toward worship? Which set of eyes is dominant within your church?

2. Before looking at the church, let's apply this chapter personally. Which of the nineteen principles outlined in this chapter describe your attitude toward worship? These attitudes will help in dealing with others who worship God differently.

3. Which principles outlined in this chapter do you struggle with personally? Identify one or two principles you can work on in the next few months to help you become more tolerant of other approaches to worship.

4. Now, let's ask the same questions about the church. Which statements describe the way most people in your church approach varieties in worship? Take time to encourage the church in these areas that they might continue to build on their strengths.

5. Which principles outlined are struggles for those in your church? As a worship leader, how can you help the people of God grow in this area?

Worship Project

As you evaluate your church in light of the nineteen principles outlined by Towns, there may be several that are a source of concern to you as you seek to mature the church in the discipline and ministry of worship. Make a list of these concerns and prioritize them in order of importance. Then take the first item on the list and begin developing a strategy to help your church grow in this area.

As a group, take time to brainstorm for ideas that might be useful in addressing the problem you have chosen. When you complete your list, sift through the ideas to find several workable ideas. Sometimes, even a bad idea can be adjusted to become a good and workable idea. Then, prepare a strategy that will help you address the worship concern in your church.

Session Twelve

This is it! We have come to the end of our study of worship. In this final chapter, Towns discusses the future of worship. As we work through this final chapter together, we will attempt to project a future for worship in our church.

Study Questions

1. Towns writes, "The core of worship can never change." As you begin this session, make a list of the unchanging essentials of worship. Be careful not to confuse your preferences in worship style with the heart of worship itself.

2. Towns begins this final chapter discussing several current trends in worship. Which of these trends have begun to influence the way you worship God in your church? Which trends would you like to see have a greater influence in your church?

3. The second part of this chapter describes changes in church. How is your church different from the church in which you were raised? If your church is more than ten years old, what changes have taken place in the history of your church? How do these changes impact the way you worship God?

4. Towns concludes this chapter with a warning when he writes, "Why is it when leaders get their hands on religion, one of the first things they want to do is to use religion to control people?" Has this been a problem in your church? If so, what steps can be taken to correct this problem? If not, what safeguards should be put in place to prevent this from becoming a problem in the future?

5. How has your understanding of worship changed as you have worked through our study of *Putting an End to Worship Wars*? Identify two new insights you have gained in this study series. How are these insights impacting the way you worship God?

Worship Project

God is still seeking worshipers (John 4:24). As you have worked through this study series, you have evaluated your own church in various contexts. As you conclude this study, use the following questions to measure your church's health and growth in worship.

1. What does your church do well in worshiping God? Build on this strength.

2. In what areas of worship is your church making progress? Keep up the good work.

3. What is the single most significant concern in worship that needs to be addressed in your church in the next year? May God grant you grace as you mature in this area.

The Lord bless you and your church as you prepare to "bless the Lord" in worship.

Notes

1. Jack Hayford, *Worship His Majesty* (Waco, Tex.: Word Books, 1987), 88. This theme of a reformation of worship, in addition to a reformation of doctrine, is a constant theme of this book. Hayford would like to see a worship form like the Renewal Church (see chap. 7) in all churches.

Chapter 1

1. Elmer Towns, *Ten of Today's Most Innovative Churches* (Ventura, Calif.: Regal Books, 1990). The ideas of chapter 1 in this book are an expansion of *Introduction to Ten Innovative Churches*, 9–18, 193–209.

2. Ibid., 193–209. The six worship forms are first introduced and described.

Chapter 3

1. Elmer Towns, general editor, *A Practical Encyclopedia of Evangelism and Church Growth* (Ventura, Calif.: Regal Books, 1996). See "Church Growth Movement, Beginning of," 76; and "Church Growth Definitions," 72.

2. Ibid. "Homogeneous Unit and People Movement," 264.

3. Ibid. "Homogeneous Unit Principle," 268.

4. Ibid. "Homogeneous Unit Principle: Application," 268.

5. Ibid. "Barriers to Evangelism and Church Growth Definitions," 27; and "Barriers to Evangelism and Church Growth: Description," 29.

6. Elmer Towns, *Ten of Today's Most Innovative Churches* (Ventura, Calif.: Regal Books, 1990), 207.

7. Towns, *Encyclopedia of Evangelism*, "Cross-Cultural Evangelism," 122.

8. Donald McGavran, *The Bridges of God* (New York: Friendship Press, 1955).

9. Towns, *Encyclopedia of Evangelism*, "Church Growth Movement: Beginning of," 76.

10. Ibid., "Church Growth: Social Sciences," 78.

11. Ibid., "Motivation for Evangelism and Church Growth," 303. This article summarizes the dissertation of Flavil Yeakley.

Chapter 4

1. Robert Wenz, *Room for God, A Worship Challenge for a Church Growth and Market Era* (Grand Rapids: Baker Book House, 1994).

2. Marva Dawn, *Reaching Out Without Dumbing Down: A Theology for Worship for the Turn-of-the-Century Church* (Grand Rapids: William B. Eerdmans Publishing Co., 1995). Marva Dawn is a church musician and theologian (Ph.D. in Christian Ethics and the Scriptures from Notre Dame).

3. Ibid., 6–7.
4. Ibid., 41.
5. Ibid., 17.
6. Ibid., 54.
7. Robert R. Redman Jr., "Friendly Fire, Evangelical Critics Take Aim at Contemporary Worship," *Worship Leader*, November/December, 1995, 35.
8. Dawn, *Reaching Out*. See chapter 6, 105ff.

Chapter 5

1. Elmer Towns, *The Ten Largest Sunday Schools and What Makes Them Grow* (Grand Rapids: Baker Book House, 1969). The churches in this book represented several denominational affiliations, but were all evangelistic in thrust.
2. Towns, *America's Fastest Growing Churches* (Nashville: Impact Books, 1972). The churches in this book were all independent Baptist in affiliation and represented the Evangelistic Church paradigm.

Chapter 6

1. Ray Stedman, *Body Life* (Glendale, Calif.: Regal Books, 1972), 86.
2. Haddon Robinson, *Biblical Preaching: The Development and Delivery of Expository Messages* (Grand Rapids: Baker Book House, 1980), 20.
3. Gary Inrig, *Life in His Body* (Wheaton: Harold Shaw, 1975), 43.

Chapter 7

1. Jack W. Hayford, *Worship His Majesty* (Waco, Texas: Word Books Publisher, 1987), 144.
2. Ibid., 45.

Chapter 8

1. Ray Stedman, "Church Life," *United Evangelical Action*, April 1967, 27–28.
2. Gene Getz, *Sharpening the Focus of the Church* (Chicago: Moody Press, 1974), 38.

Chapter 10

1. Arthur Flake, *Building a Standard Sunday School* (Nashville: Convention Press, 1922), 19.

Bibliography

Allen, Ronald, and Gordon Borrow. *Worship: Rediscovering the Missing Jewel.* Portland, Oreg.: Multnomah Press, 1982. Written to help churches rediscover the jewel of worship in the local church setting, the book defines and describes various aspects of the worship service and provides practical guidelines for those responsible for planning worship services.

Bartow, Charles. *Effective Speech Communication in Leading Worship.* Nashville: Abingdon Press, 1988. Written from a liturgical perspective, this book includes practical advice for worship leaders to help them communicate more effectively.

Baxter, J. Sidlow. *The God You Should Know.* San Bernardino, Calif.: Here's Life, 1984.

————. *Rethinking Our Priorities.* Grand Rapids: Zondervan Publishing House, 1974.

Benson, Dennis C. *Creative Worship in Youth Ministry.* Loveland, Colo.: Group Books, 1985. Helpful in planning worship times for youth meetings.

Best, Harold M. *Music Through the Eyes of Faith.* San Francisco: HarperCollins Publishers, 1993. The dean of the Wheaton Conservatory of Music presents his philosophy of music, worship, and aesthetics.

Bolte, Chuck, and Paul McCusker. *Youth Ministry Drama and Comedy.* Loveland, Colo.: Group Books, 1987. Valuable for those involved in developing drama ministries as part of their worship services.

Carrol, Joseph. *How to Worship Jesus Christ.* Chicago: Moody Press, 1991. Focusing on personal worship, the writer discusses practical concepts of worship drawn from Revelation and other parts of Scripture.

Carson, D. A. *Worship: Adoration and Action.* Grand Rapids: Baker Book House, 1993. Two theological essays on worship, as well as in-depth reflections on current worship practices in South America, South Africa, and Europe.

Carson, Herbert M. *Hallelujah: Christian Worship.* Welwyn, England: Evangelical Press, 1980. Addresses the theology and practice of worship from a British perspective.

Christensen, James L. *Don't Waste Your Time in Worship.* Old Tappan, N.J.: Flemming H. Revell, 1978. Attempts to help the worshiper make the worship time in church more meaningful.

Cornwall, Judson. *Let Us Worship.* South Plainfield, N.J.: Bridge Publications, 1983. A pentecostal theologian explains the concept of the Journey into the Holy of Holies, and makes a clear distinction between praise and worship.

Cullman, Oscar. *Early Christian Worship.* Philadelphia: Westminster Press, 1978.

Dawn, Marva. *Reaching Out without Dumbing Down: A Theology for Worship for the Turn-of-the-Century Church.* Grand Rapids: Eerdmans, 1995. Defends traditional liturgical worship and is critical of contemporary praise music in worship.

Davies, J. G. *The Westminster Dictionary of Worship.* Philadelphia: The Westminster Press, 1972. Written from a liturgical perspective, a valuable resource on the history of worship, meaning of various worship terms, and the practice of worship among various denominations.

Dobson, J. O. *Worship.* London: S.C.M. Press, 1941.

Eskew, Harry and Hugh T. McElrath. *Sing with Understanding: An Introduction to Christian Hymnody.* 2d ed. Nashville: Church Street Publishers, 1996. A seminary text in hymnology that is helpful for those responsible for selecting hymns for the worship service.

Flynn, Leslie. *Worship: Together We Celebrate.* Wheaton, Ill.: Victor Books, 1983.

Gaddy, C. Welton. *The Gift of Worship.* Nashville: Broadman Press, 1992. A Southern Baptist pastor professor presents his synthesis of worship in a nontechnical style. An approach rich with pastoral observation and experience.

Gentile, Ernest B. *Worship God!: Exploring the Dynamics of Psalmic Worship.* Portland, Oreg.: Bible Temple Publishing, 1994. Urging a return to psalmic worship that incorporates the whole person.

Gibbs, Alfred D. *Worship, The Christian's Highest Occupation.* Kansas City, Kans.: Walterick Publications, n.d.

Hahn, Ferdinand. *The Worship of the Early Church.* Philadelphia: Fortress Press, 1973.

Hayford, Jack. *Worship His Majesty.* Dallas: Word, 1987. A standard work by the author of several popular worship choruses outlining his view that worship is the key to people recovering God's intended purpose for their lives and having personal needs met by God.

Hayford, Jack, with John Killinger and Howard Stevenson. *Mastering Worship.* Portland, Oreg.: Multnomah Press/Christianity Today, 1990. Written by three respected worship leaders representing three different evangelical denominations, this book describes both personal and public aspects of worship. The chapter "Adding Creativity without Losing the Congregation" may prove helpful to many pastors seeking to be innovative in planning their worship services.

Hustad, Donald P. *Jubilate! Church Music in the Evangelical Tradition.* Carol Stream, Ill.: Hope Publishing Company, 1981. A well-researched volume discussing the history of evangelical worship in various contexts with an emphasis on the role of culture and its influence on various worship expressions.

————. *Jubilate II: Church Music in Worship and Renewal.* Carol Stream, Ill.: Hope Publishing Company, 1993. Broad coverage of all aspects of mainstream, evangelical church music and worship. Strong historical emphasis.

Johansson, Calvin M. *Music & Ministry: A Biblical Counterpoint.* Peabody, Mass.: Hendrickson Publishers, 1984. Passionately written. Relates music and ministry to the basic Christian doctrines.

Keffer, Lois. *Creative Worship Ideas.* Loveland, Colo.: Group Books, 1992. Describes seventy approaches to involving youth in worship.

Kendall, R. T. *Before the Throne: A Comprehensive Guide to the Importance and Practice of Worship.* Nashville: Broadman & Holman, 1993. The pastor of London's Westminster Chapel discusses worship from a Free Church perspective.

Kendrick, Graham. *Learning to Worship as a Way of Life.* Minneapolis, Minn.: Bethany House, 1985. A study of the relationship between personal and corporate worship with an emphasis on the effect of worship on one's personal lifestyle.

————. *Ten Worshipping Churches.* Essex, Great Britain: MARC Europe & British Church Growth Association, 1987. The stories of ten British churches and the struggles they encountered as they changed the corporate worship patterns in their churches.

Kreider, Eleanor. *Enter His Gates: Fitting Worship Together.* Scottsdale, Pa.: Herald Press, 1990. Deals with preparing a worship experience satisfying to both God and the worshiper.

Liesch, Barry. *People in the Presence of God: Models and Directions for Worship.* Grand Rapids: Zondervan, 1988. Views worship from a contemporary perspective with many practical suggestions for enhancing and transforming worship in the church. Views five scriptural worship models of worship. An emphasis on the acts in worship.

Lind, Millard C. *Biblical Foundations for Christian Worship.* Scottsdale, Pa.: Herald Press, 1973. A brief study on the biblical theology of worship.

MacArthur, John. *The Ultimate Priority.* Chicago: Moody Press, 1983. Based on a sermon series, the fourteen chapters of this book discuss various aspects of the biblical teaching on worship in both the Old and New Testaments.

Martin, Ralph P. *Worship in the Early Church.* Grand Rapids: Eerdmans, 1975. An analysis of the theology and practice of New Testament worship.

————. *The Worship of God: Some Theological, Pastoral and Practical Reflections.* Grand Rapids: Eerdmans, 1982. A study of the theological reason for various worship practices.

Maxwell, William D. *A History of Christian Worship.* Grand Rapids: Baker Book House, 1936, 1982. A survey of the history of worship with emphasis on worship in the Reformation era.

Morey, Robert. *Worship Is All of Life.* Camp Hill, Pa: Christian Publications, 1984. A study of personal, family, and public worship.

Morgenthaller, Sally. *Worship Evangelism.* Grand Rapids: Zondervan Publishing House, 1995.

Ortlund, Anne. *Up with Worship: How to Quit Playing Church.* Ventura, Calif.: Regal Books, 1982. A practical handbook designed to help improve various technical aspects of the worship service.

Pass, David P. *Music and the Church: A Theology of Church Music.* Nashville: Broadman Press, 1989. Music as a communication system that addresses proclamation, fellowship, and worship in the church.

Peterson, Randy. *Giving to the Giver: Worship that Pleases God.* Wheaton, Ill.: Tyndale Publishing House, 1990. Study of various words describing worship and examples of worship in Scripture.

Peterson, David. *Engaging with God: A Biblical Theology of Worship.* Grand Rapids: Eerdmans, 1993. A study of worship as a total life orientation, an "engagement with God."

Rayburn, Robert G. *O Come, Let Us Worship: Corporate Worship in the Evangelical Church.* Grand Rapids: Baker Book House, 1980. A study of the biblical teaching on worship from a sacramental perspective.

Saliers, Don E. *Worship and Spirituality.* Philadelphia: Westminster Press, 1984.

Sanders, J. Oswald. *Enjoying Intimacy with God.* Chicago: Moody Press, 1980. Includes a chapter addressing worship as a means to achieving greater intimacy with God.

Schaper, Robert N. *In His Presence: Appreciating Your Worship Tradition.* Nashville: Thomas Nelson, 1984. A study of the history of worship, especially in the liturgical tradition.

Segler, Franklin M. and C. Randall Bradley. *Understanding, Preparing for, and Practicing Christian Worship.* 2d ed. Nashville: Broadman & Holman, 1996. A traditional approach to worship from a congregational church perspective.

Senn, Frank C. *Christian Worship and Its Cultural Setting.* Philadelphia: Fortress Press, 1983.

Sheldon, Robin, ed. *In Spirit and Truth: Exploring Directions in Music in Worship Today.* London: Hodder & Stoughton, 1989. Fascinating essays revealing the tensions between traditional and contemporary church music in Great Britain today.

Sheppard, Lancelot. *True Worship.* Baltimore: The Helicon Press, 1963.

Stacker, Joe R. and Wesley Forbis. *Authentic Worship: Exalting God and Reaching People.* Nashville: Convention Press, 1990. Includes practical ideas on planning aspects of worship, including advice on developing a blended worship service.

Thielen, Martin. *Getting Ready for Sunday: A Practical Guide for Worship Planning.* Nashville: Broadman Press, 1989. Beginning with the premise that worship is an encounter with God, this book provides numerous suggestions to help guide a worship team through the process of planning meaningful worship services.

Tozer, A. W. *Whatever Happened to Worship?* Camp Hill, Pa.: Christian Publications, 1985. Based on a series of sermons on the theme "Worship: The Chief End of Man."

Wardel, Terry Howard. *Exalt Him: Designing Dynamic Worship Services.* Camp Hill, Pa.: Christian Publications, 1988. Practical book on designing worship services.

Webber, Robert E. *Topical Encyclopedia of Christian Worship.* Nashville: Star Song, 1992. A seven-volume encyclopedia on worship.

———. *Worship Is a Verb.* Nashville: Abbott-Martyn, 1992. Includes eight principles for a highly participatory worship service.

———. *Worship Old and New.* Grand Rapids: Zondervan, 1982. History and theology of worship from a liturgical perspective.

———. *The Complete Library of Christian Worship.* Nashville: Star Song Publishing Group, 1993, seven volumes. The most ambitious and comprehensive volume available on Christian worship. Contributions from over 60 denominations and 600 writers.

Wenz, Robert. *Room for God, A Worship Challenge for a Church Growth and Market Era.* Grand Rapids: Baker Book House, 1994. Suggests the church has gone beyond sensitivity to believers and has accommodated the unsaved at the cost of violating biblical values.

Westermeyer, Paul. *The Church Musician.* San Francisco: Harper & Row, 1988. Lutheran. Views the central role of the church musician as a cantor, and analyzes the pastor/musician relationship.

White, James. *A Brief History of Christian Worship.* Nashville: Abingdon Press, 1993. A historical survey of worship written from a liturgical perspective.

———. *Introduction to Christian Worship.* Nashville: Abingdon Press, 1990. Deals with the meaning of Christian worship and aspects of the worship service in the liturgical tradition.

————. *Protestant Worship: Traditions in Transition.* Louisville, Ky.: Westminister/John Knox Press, 1989. Insightful analysis of the major Christian worship traditions from the Reformation to the present.

Wiersbe, Warren W. *Real Worship: It Will Transform Your Life.* Nashville: Oliver-Nelson Books, 1986. Practical insights into both personal and corporate worship and the need to integrate both.

————. *Classic Sermons on Worship.* Grand Rapids: Kregel, 1988. Sermons on worship from various nineteenth-century preachers.

Willimon, William H. *Preaching and Leading Worship.* Philadelphia: Westminster Press, 1984.

————. *Worship As Pastoral Care.* Nashville: Abingdon Press, 1979.